An American

HERO

An American HERO

ONE MAN'S LEGACY OF FATHERHOOD AND FAITH

BY
THOMAS DAVIS JR.
WITH JACK WATTS

Forefront
B O O K S

Published by Forefront Books, Nashville, Tennessee.

Distributed by Simon & Schuster.

Library of Congress Control Number: 2024926615

Print ISBN: 978-1-63763-395-3

E-book ISBN: 978-1-63763-396-0

Cover Design by Bruce Gore, Gore Studio, Inc.
Interior Design by PerfecType, Nashville, TN
Printed in the United States of America

The purpose of life
is a life of purpose.

—ROBERT BYRNE

Contents

Preface

I lost my dad when he was still a very young man, just fifty-three years old. Because his passing was so sudden, entirely unexpected, it was a devastating blow to everybody in our family. He was my hero, a presence in my life so large that no one has ever been able to replace him. I suspect many have similar feelings. You only have one dad. As is so often the case, my father became even more important after his death. What he taught me, especially concerning lessons about how to be a good man, has guided me ever since.

As a result, from the time of his tragic passing, as one of my purposes in life, I've made a commitment to write a book about this larger-than-life man. During his brief tenure on earth, and even more so after his death, his words, his leadership, and his example have provided me with inspiration. I've looked to his words to influence me, and they have, including times where I've had to go through some very rough waters. His leadership, even from the grave, has provided me with the prudence I've needed to make wise, sound decisions. My hope is that I can pass on the lessons I've learned to those who read *An American Hero*.

Without his fatherly mentoring, I doubt I would have become as successful as I have. In fact, I'm certain of it. Although I've made plenty of mistakes along the way, because success is almost never a straight line upward, the character qualities I've internalized from being his only son have allowed me to make far fewer miscues than I would have on my own.

Now, as I am nearing the end of my business career and approaching full retirement, I want to pass on what I have learned, but I don't want to bore readers by enumerating sappy platitudes. Instead, because I learned my lessons from real-life experiences, I want to pass them along in like manner. At times, my dad handled things in ways that modern-day parents wouldn't, but they were effective in teaching me the lesson I needed to learn. I've chosen to include these stories.

I believe that, as I recount the story of the man who inspired me, the reader can learn what I have in exactly the same way. My hope is that the tale I am about to tell will have lasting benefit to you. That's my purpose. As much as anything, *An American Hero* is the story of my dad's life. Let me assure you: it is an interesting, compelling tale—one that will keep you fully engaged. Except for some creative license with dialogue, the story is completely true to life.

When I began to develop the book's contents, it quickly became clear that to provide full justice regarding who James Thomas Davis Sr. was, I would need to tell the story of my grandfather, my siblings and their children, and my own story as well. So, instead of this book focusing exclusively on my father's life, the memoir I intended has turned into a four-generation saga. Starting from the time Thomas Davis came into this world, his unique story reveals not just how influential my father's life has been on me personally, but also on the rest of my family and many others as well.

An American Hero is actually a tapestry, an intricate weaving of thoughts and actions that have been impactful for more than a hundred years. My hope is that you will also draw inspiration from my father's life and legacy along the way.

INTEGRITY, PURPOSE, AND EXCELLENCE

*There are really three parts to the creative process.
First there is inspiration, then there is the execution,
and finally there is the release.*
—EDDIE VAN HALEN

My name is Thomas Davis Jr., but most people call me Tommy. As far as a career is concerned, I've done many things. More than any other line of work, I've been in the construction business. I've been pretty good at it, too, achieving a substantial measure of success. Some might say I'm a perfect example of the American dream coming true.

Now in my early seventies, I continue to work because I love what I do. I'm not a workaholic, though. I've learned to stop along the way, smell the roses, and enjoy the fruits of my labor. My wife, Buttercup, makes certain that I do.

Life is good for my wife and me. Now semiretired, we have a great time eating out, traveling, and spending quality time with our friends and family. We're very social, especially her.

Having achieved prosperity, we live in a lovely, well-appointed home in Boca Raton, Florida. Not all that far from Mar-a-Lago, our home is located where many of the most well-to-do and influential people in America live. With both of us in good health, we enjoy the benefits of having reached the American dream.

Although I worked long hours and many years to become successful, experiencing several reversals along the way, we now live in an era in which being diligent, hardworking, and steadfast in purpose are no longer considered praise-worthy. For many in the United States, striving to achieve excellence is no longer lauded. Instead, it is ridiculed.

In this upside-down way of thinking, being fruitful has become reviled. The qualities necessary to achieve success are no longer considered estimable. Instead, they are scorned in favor of elevating mediocrity. Younger generations, the Gen Xers, Millennials, and Gen Zers, have an entirely different interpretation of what successful businessmen like me are really like. Criticizing us, they consider us to be callous, self-seeking, greedy villains. They refuse to believe we have achieved the fruits of our success legitimately. Dismissing our hard work and the values we've internalized to reach our goals, they believe our success is based on "white privilege."

Because of this privilege, the narrative asserts, we don't deserve the wealth we've accumulated. According to this Progressive way of thinking, the deck of cards has been stacked in our favor and against others. According to this worldview, we're oppressors. They insist it has always been this way, going all the way back to America's founding. Holding us in contempt, they reason we have used others unfairly. Having done so, our wealth doesn't rightfully belong to us. This makes us the benefactors of ill-gotten gains.

Millions of young Americans fervently believe this perspective to be true. Rather than aspiring to emulate what people like me have accomplished, gaining the same level of prosperity for themselves through diligence, they repudiate every aspect of the American dream. They resent people like me for being successful. They do this without having the slightest clue about who we are or what we are really like. They just assume that we don't deserve what we have, that what we have accumulated has been gained illicitly.

Embittered by the perceived disparity in our favor, they are convinced the system is rigged for us and against them. Repudiating the Judeo-Christian work ethic in its entirety—which is based on a worldview that has been adhered to by nearly all Americans since the days of the Pilgrims and the Puritans—woke Progressives now consider being an affluent white male a shameful thing. Consequently, men like me are depicted as unworthy of respect.

Based on this viewpoint, there is nothing heroic about me or others like me. Analyzing this perspective, the question needs to be asked: Is it possible that their world-view is accurate? Are we oppressors? Do their pronouncements have merit? Are we what they consider us to be, or are we something entirely different?

To begin with, even though the Progressive world-view is puzzling, it doesn't anger me that many think this way, especially naïve young people. It's what they have been taught.

The problem is, I don't believe that what woke Progressives espouse is accurate or true. It's certainly not in my case, and it's probably not for many others as well. Our stories don't fit the narrative they have created for us. Mine definitely doesn't. To understand who I am and what has made me successful, one must first know and understand my dad and my grandfather's stories. This requires taking a deeper look at two earlier generations.

Generational sin is discussed in the Bible. It's described in several places in the Pentateuch—the first five books of the Bible. There is a verse that says the sins of the fathers are passed down to the third and fourth generations (Exodus 20:5). If this is true, and I'm convinced that it is, then the inverse is also true. It would have to be. The blessings of the fathers are also passed down to the children, the grandchildren, the great-grandchildren, and to subsequent generations after that.

These multiplied generational blessings, which go back to the settlers, are what have made the United States the greatest, most prosperous nation in the history of the world. These blessings are what transpired at the macro level, benefitting the entire nation.

To know my story, which is a story at the micro level, you must understand that my blessings weren't material. They were the values I learned and internalized from being my father's son. I didn't start out as a wealthy man. When I began my career as a young man, I certainly wasn't financially set for life or even close to it. Despite not being wealthy, I was blessed to have developed many estimable character qualities. These qualities were bestowed on me by my father.

Often learning lessons the hard way, like so many do, significant positive character qualities were instilled in me through my father's diligent efforts. He poured into me what he had to give: not money, but valuable life lessons. He did this for my three sisters as well.

Although I didn't start out affluent, I was rich nonetheless. I possessed a sense of purpose, a sense of direction, and a highly defined awareness of what was right and what was wrong. I knew who I was and who I aspired to be. Becoming wealthy was a natural byproduct of all of this.

I was my father's son. More than anything, I wanted to make him proud of me. I still do, even though he has been gone for more than half a century. I continue to seek his approval posthumously.

The character qualities I gained from being the son of Thomas Davis Sr. are what positioned me to succeed, not being the beneficiary of inherited wealth. White privilege was never involved, as *An American Hero* will attest.

What my father had to give—integrity, purpose, and a righteous worldview—he gave, but the questions need to be asked: How did my father obtain these qualities?

Where did he get them? Where did they originate? Did he obtain them from his father, or could there be another, more interesting explanation?

I suspect you might know the answer. It's how he gained these qualities that makes the following story so interesting. It's why I have written *An American Hero*.

I am who I am because of who my father was.

More than any other thing, what follows is the story of an American hero from the Greatest Generation. Thomas Davis Sr. was unique, and so was his life.

This is where the story begins. It started on a hot summer day in August, shortly after the end of the Great War, in the deep woods of Hanging Dog Mountain, located in the Appalachians in rural North Carolina.

> *I know whom I have believed, and I am*
> *convinced that He is able to protect what I*
> *have entrusted to Him until that day.*
>
> (2 Timothy 1:12)

Chapter 1

★ ★ ★

HANGING DOG MOUNTAIN

Believe in yourself!
Have faith in your abilities!
Without a humble but reasonable
confidence in your own powers
you cannot be successful or happy.
—Norman Vincent Peale

I n August 1921, just a few days after President Warren G. Harding commemorated the 300th anniversary of the Pilgrims' landing at Plymouth Rock—perhaps even on the same day that the Italian opera star Enrico Caruso died— my father was born on Hanging Dog Mountain in rural North Carolina. This sparsely populated area in the Appalachians is just a few miles east of the Tennessee border.

My dad, a true son of this mountainous region, was very proud of where he was born. Whenever he would tell someone that he came into the world from such an unusual place, his eyes would light up. He loved the surprised looks on the faces of his audience. This always made him smile.

Hanging Dog Mountain was a name created by a Cherokee Indian. It was where a dog had been rescued from the hanging debris on a tributary overlooking the Hiawassee River. My father never bothered to mention this part of the story—that the dog was rescued. Instead, he allowed the listeners to draw their own conclusion, which they inevitably did. That they thought some poor animal had been hanged delighted my father, even though that's not what really happened.

During this era, it wasn't unusual for families to be quite large. My father's family was no exception. He was the middle son of James Edgar Davis and his wife, May Bell Palmer Davis. When there are numerous children in a household, older siblings often do as much parenting as the mother and father. In my dad's case, it was the family dog, a boxer, who was responsible for him, especially for his safety. As a toddler, my father liked to wander around outside, often venturing toward the dirt road. When he did, the boxer would grab ahold of my dad's diaper or shirt and drag him back to safety. The dog was so proficient at guarding Jimmy, which is what everybody called my dad, that whenever he would go outside, May Bell would make certain the dog accompanied him. She knew that even though her son was an adventurous toddler, the dog would keep him safe.

When Edgar and May Bell married, though they were from Appalachia, they were quite well off financially.

Edgar had inherited a great deal of money from his parents, perhaps as much as $1 million. This was an astronomical sum a hundred years ago. It would be valued at a little more than $15 million in today's dollars. This financial cushion was sufficient for the Davis family to live comfortably, without any financial worries for the rest of their lives—and perhaps for their children's lives as well.

Being the beneficiary of such a fortune was the good news. The bad news was my grandfather was a gambler and a heavy drinker. A profligate by nature, he eventually lost everything he'd inherited. Obviously a poor gambler, one might think he should have been smart enough to stop, but he never did. His narcissism and his addiction drove him relentlessly downward, but that's not all. His misfortune didn't end by wasting a fortune.

He had other issues as well. A man given to the pursuit of vice, Edgar wasn't constitutionally built to withstand even a modicum of adversity. With a penchant for dissipation, when a crisis arose in the family that required strong leadership, he didn't have the necessary character qualities to weather the storm. When tough times arrived, he refused to be the one who was negatively impacted. Instead, he passed the buck, forcing his children to be the ones to suffer—and suffer they did.

Edgar Davis's actions in the face of calamity negatively impacted his children's future for the remainder of their lives. In the South, when someone behaves like my grandfather did, people say, "He's just sorry." In my grandfather's case, no truer words could have been spoken. Edgar Davis was a "sorry" man.

The crux of the family crisis involved my grandmother's health. When my father was still quite young, no older than five, his mom was diagnosed with a brain tumor. With medical treatment for such a condition in its infancy in the 1920s, there was little available to fight her disease. Consequently, May Bell's health deteriorated quickly. Within a year she died, leaving her husband alone to raise a family of four children.

Given a regrettable situation like this, some men rally to the cause, doing whatever is necessary to meet the needs of their children. A few go to extraordinary lengths to raise them properly. My grandfather wasn't such a man. Not only was he incapable of doing what was necessary, he had no desire to even try.

He was unwilling to play the hand he had been dealt, choosing instead to fold his cards.

With May Bell's parents having passed years earlier, Edgar was all his children had. He knew this, but it wasn't a responsibility he was willing to embrace. It was a burden that required unloading. His children were an unwanted encumbrance, adversely affecting his lifestyle. They were an infringement on the lewd lifestyle he desired to lead.

Making the decision to walk away instead of manning up to his responsibilities courageously, Edgar refused to do what was necessary to keep his family intact. Instead, he chose the exact opposite. Just a year before the stock market crashed, launching the Great Depression, my grandfather put all three of his sons into the car one morning to take them on a six-hour, four-hundred-mile trek across North Carolina. Eventually arriving in Oxford, a small town located forty miles north of Raleigh and ten miles south of the Virginia border, Edgar Davis had no qualms about what he was about to do.

His sons were clueless regarding their impending fate. Having no idea why they had been in the car for so long, the boys did not want to incur their father's wrath by expressing their curiosity. They knew better than to ask where they were going, much less why. Despite the length of the trip, they did their best to behave, refusing to cause a ruckus in the back seat.

Arriving at their destination, Edgar Davis directed his three sons to get out of the car. Then, refusing to be honest about what was about to happen, after unloading their sparse clothing from the trunk, he simply got back into his car, put it in gear, and drove off, leaving his three sons, all under seven years old, to fend for themselves. He left them at the front door of the Masonic Home for Children at Oxford.

The Masonic Home was an orphanage, the first one in North Carolina. It's still in operation today, having housed more than eleven thousand children over the years. Founded in 1873, just a few years after the end of the Civil War, its existence was necessary because there were so many fatherless children due to wartime casualties. The need for such a home was overwhelming after the Great War. It continued to be necessary during the Great Depression, which began shortly after my father and his brothers arrived at the Masonic Home.

To my six-year-old father, that his dad would abandon him, just a few months after the death of his mother, must have been overwhelming. At such a young age, how could a small child even understand what was happening? The answer is, he couldn't have.

Over time, however, my dad came to realize exactly what had transpired. Along with his two brothers, he was forced to come to grips with being abandoned. Discarded and cast aside, the three Davis boys had no option other than to admit the truth about what had happened to them, but it was a difficult pill to swallow.

When Edgar Davis deserted my father, as well as his older brother, Frank, and his younger brother, Robert, all three eventually realized that their father wasn't coming back. At first, as they watched for his car to pull into the orphanage's driveway each day; they felt certain he would return. Eager for him to do so, they were vigilant. Like loyal dogs, they waited patiently, but he never came back.

But that's not all. He never even came to visit them—not once. When he dropped them off, they were on their own. He was through with them. Edgar never called, nor did he write. He never sent them any money either, not even when he'd had a good night gambling.

Edgar considered them to be an unwanted burden and was grateful to be rid of them. Out of sight, they were also out of mind. Now divested of his three sons, Edgar was free to pursue his calling—drinking, gambling, and womanizing.

My dad's younger sister, Mary Jo, experienced a similar fate. Stricken with polio as an infant, she required specialized attention. Following the same pattern, my grandfather left his infant daughter at an orphanage where her medical needs could be addressed. This was a plus for her even though she was several years younger than my dad. The negative part was that she was all alone. Having to deal with the most dreaded disease of the era, Mary Jo, an unwanted child, was both motherless and fatherless.

At least my father had his two brothers. He wasn't isolated. As the reality of their situation became clear, their fraternal bond intensified. Although they had no parents, and never would again, they had each other. This produced a tight, unassailable bond among them that lasted throughout their lives.

The normal fighting and squabbling that exists between siblings, especially boys, was not their experience. Knowing that it was them against the world, they parented themselves. Instead of allowing their situation to destroy them, however, they refused to be deterred. In spite of everything, they thrived.

Abandoned at such an early age as the country entered the Great Depression, my dad and his brothers spent more than ten years at the Oxford orphanage. With scarcity plaguing the nation, one can only imagine the level of destitution Edgar's three sons must have experienced.

Meanwhile, my grandfather found another woman to bed and to take care of his other needs. Eventually marrying her, the couple had several children. Essentially, Edgar replaced his first family in its entirety. His second batch of children might have done well if their dad had learned his lesson about drinking and gambling, but he never did.

I saw for myself that he hadn't when I was still quite young. Because we—especially my older sister—hounded

Dad so much, he took us on a road trip to visit his father. Not having met my grandfather before, or even heard much about him, I was definitely curious. Like any kid would be, I was anxious to meet him.

When I did, I was stunned. Immediately revolted walking into the shack where he lived, which was deep in the woods, I was repulsed by how filthy everything was. To have come from such wealth only to end up in such abject squalor was something I will never forget. My grandfather's life was like a sermon illustration about how to destroy your life. Everything was dirty; I didn't even want to sit down.

Even though we only stayed for a few hours, I couldn't wait to leave. What bothered me most was the smell. Rancid and acrid, it was sickening. I breathed through my mouth the entire time I was there. To this day, I remain sickened by the remembrance of that odor. I can still smell it nearly two-thirds of a century later.

Leading the lifestyle he did, my grandfather should have died young, but he didn't. He lived a normal lifespan, dying an old man. When informed of his death, my father refused to attend Edgar's funeral. Others coaxed him to go, thinking it would provide him with a measure of closure, but my father, who loathed hypocrisy in any form, adamantly refused. He didn't feel any grief for the man who had betrayed him and his siblings. He refused to pretend otherwise.

As I think about it, I don't believe any of Edgar's other children, none of May Bell's offspring, attended their father's funeral, but I'm not certain about that.

★ ★ ★

Life at the orphanage was rough for Edgar's children. Never pleasant, it was austere by nature. There was no warmth provided by the adults who were paid to take care of the orphans. For them, looking after the children was just a job. There was no love bestowed, no comfort or affirmation provided. Any validation that came my father's way was delivered by his brothers and some of the other orphans. The life my father lived at the Masonic Home for Children at Oxford was not unlike what Oliver Twist experienced in the Charles Dickens novel, but at least Jimmy and his brothers were housed and fed. They weren't left to fend for themselves on the street.

Even as young as they were when they first arrived, they were given significant responsibilities. During the cold winters, the boys were required to get up before dawn to light the fires in the kitchen. They also had to light the fireplaces throughout the facility to warm it before the caretakers arose.

The only adult who took a personal interest in my father and his brothers was the Black caretaker, Mr. Jack. Struggling to survive the Great Depression, the orphanage grew most of its own produce. It was Mr. Jack's responsibility to ensure that the crops were bountiful. It was my dad's job to help him, but this was a labor of love. While working, he and Mr. Jack would talk, laugh, and have a great time doing everything that was necessary for the orphans to survive.

When he later spoke about his life at the home, the only aspect of it my father considered pleasant, other than

growing up with his brothers, was the time he spent with
Mr. Jack. Full of life, this older gentleman was the only
adult who ever showed that he cared about my father.

One might expect that growing up like this might
have made my father bitter, but it never did. He never
considered himself to be a victim, nor did he bemoan his
situation. Although he had been dealt a tough hand, even
from early childhood he understood that he was required
to make the best of it.

This was the first lesson I learned from him: Never
whine and never lament. Instead, regardless of your situation, if you can't change it, try to make the best of it.
When life gets you down, which it inevitably does, never
wallow in self-pity. Instead, get up, shake off the dirt, and
move forward. Always move forward.

That's what my father and his two brothers did. Despite
being raised in an orphanage, they thrived. Deprived of
the love of an intact family, what my father wanted most in
life was to have a loving family of his own. He vowed that
he would make that happen at some point.

Unlike his dissipating father, my dad would often say,
"No matter how the cards fall, you deal with the hand you are
given." Learning from him, this is exactly what I have done.

Everyone is handed adversity in
life. No one's journey is easy.
It's how they handle it that makes people unique.
KEVIN CONROY

Chapter 2

★ ★ ★

A FULL SCHOLARSHIP
TO DUKE

We must accept finite disappointment,
but never lose infinite hope.
—MARTIN LUTHER KING JR.

Although it is hard to imagine, at the tender age of six—with the Great Depression looming, bringing financial ruin to American families at an unprecedented rate and decimating the nation's economy while producing want and even famine—my father, along with his siblings, was forced to face the world fatherless and motherless. For any six-year-old, the safety and comfort of a family is their whole life. Nothing can be an adequate replacement, certainly not an orphanage.

My father was deprived of experiencing many of the essential building blocks of life. Along with his seven-year-old brother, Frank, and four-year-old brother, James, the trio were forced to endure a parentless existence.

Their sister, Mary Jo, still a toddler, would be confined to a wheelchair her entire life. Having polio from infancy, she never walked. Her situation was even more grim than theirs. She didn't even have the presence of her siblings to comfort and nurture her. All girls want to have protective big brothers. Mary Jo had three but, thanks to her heartless father's abandonment, they were never around.

Confined to live within the walls of a sanitarium, she was entirely on her own. Crippled and helpless, unable to walk or even perform routine bodily functions on her own, including essential things like tying her own shoes, her father's desertion seemed particularly callous.

It's difficult to imagine how my grandfather could have done what he did. Remorseless, feeling no guilt or recrimination for doing so, Edgar Davis dismissed his daughter's existence as an unwanted burden. He never bothered to visit her at Christmas. He didn't send her birthday cards either. Hardened narcissist that he was, life was all about him, never about his children.

All of Edgar's children experienced such a dismal beginning, with absolutely no positive prospects for the future, so one might expect that their future would be dismal, drab, and fruitless. Beginning with virtually no chance in life, having absolutely no concept of what white privilege was, having been cast off by their dad, Edgar's kids were programmed to live a life of ignominy, defeat, and poverty.

Although such an outcome would be a natural assumption to make, this is not what happened. This was not their experience. Each child, resilient in his or her own right, bucked the odds, accepted their lot in life, and moved forward, achieving significant success.

They began with nothing in the way of material possessions, nor did they have any parental support. Although unfair, even with having very little going for them, this was not enough to keep them down.

Young and resilient, they had one thing in their favor. They were Americans. They were citizens in a nation filled with opportunity, even back during the Depression. All four of them—knowing they had the ability to make something out of their lives instead of accepting the defeated future their father had prescribed for them and refusing to be a burden to society like their profligate father was—chose to look ahead with a positive attitude. Embracing optimism, they left negativity far behind.

To move forward optimistically was obviously an uphill struggle, a daily grind, but that's exactly what they did. That they, especially my father, were capable of being as accomplished as they were became an inspiration for many, including me. That none of Edgar's four children ever gave up on life, nor embraced a defeatist attitude, was inspirational.

That my grandfather would choose to waste his life, seeking pleasure while shirking his paternal responsibilities, became equally as instructive. A blackheart by nature, Edgar Davis never did an honest day's work in his life. More than any other thing, this was why he ended up defeated, living out his ignominious days in poverty and squalor.

Having squandered a fortune and the love of his children, his demise is the best example of karma I have ever witnessed. Dishonorable by nature, he chose to condemn his kids to discomfiture but, in the end, he was the one who led a shabby existence, not them.

I still think about Edgar frequently. Whenever I witness someone prospering illegitimately, often at the expense of others, I reflect on my paternal grandfather's example. When I do, I smile, knowing that anyone who believes they can achieve success through chicanery when they set out to follow an illicit path to success is only fooling themselves. It never ends well, as my grandfather's life attests.

For my dad and his two brothers, life at the orphanage was generally a bleak, joyless existence. After dinner, ice cream was never served. There were never any treats, never any luxuries of any kind. Despite this, they learned to adapt to their situation. Although they lacked the support of nurturing parents, they did have three meals a day and a roof over their heads. During the early years of the Depression, their routine was stable. Getting up early to do their mandatory chores, they set out to attend school after eating a hurried breakfast, just like all the other kids in town.

In the 1930s, life at the orphanage was governed by routine, but the children did have time to play, laugh, and horse around daily. They fought with each other too. Kids are like that. Despite everything, their enthusiasm for life was irrepressible.

Having nothing else to compare life to, kids living at the Masonic Home for Children accepted orphanage life as the norm. Without a mother and father to provide a home for them, cook their meals, and read them bedtime stories, "family" became a distant memory, replaced by years of being on their own.

With the Masonic Lodge located next door, the three boys walked past it every day on their way to school. Their education began at C. G. Credle Elementary School, where they learned to read, write, and do math. They also interacted with kids from normal homes.

Although there were several Baptist churches in town—including Oxford Baptist and First Baptist within walking distance—and an Episcopal church, too, the children's spiritual education wasn't a high priority at the orphanage. Founded and funded by Masons, most of whom enjoyed partying more than anything else, one wouldn't expect it to be.

While the boys were at school, life was normal, at least as normal as it could be for orphans. The winters were cold and the summers were hot. Back in those days, air conditioning didn't exist in the deep South, not for ordinary people who lived in Oxford. Even if it had, the orphanage wouldn't have been able to afford such a luxury. So, the kids bundled up in the winter and walked around shoeless in the summer.

The winter of 1933 was particularly cold, especially after a snowstorm. Walking to school after it snowed instead of playing on the way, my dad and his younger brother ran to avoid the cold. Once inside, they warmed themselves as best they could. By that time, Frank was already attending Butner Stem junior high where my father would attend the following year.

Dad loved school. When he was twelve and in the sixth grade, at the end of January 1933, he was totally oblivious to anything happening outside of Oxford, just like all of his classmates were. My dad was probably spending his time studying for an upcoming math test or writing a paper for English class.

While engaging in these necessary educational requirements, activities far away were shaping future events in a profound way. Things were occurring across the Atlantic Ocean, particularly in Germany, that were destined to impact my father's life. On January 30, 1933, Adolf Hitler became Germany's chancellor.

More worried about upcoming tests than anything else, my dad certainly wouldn't have paid the slightest bit of attention to anything transpiring in Europe. Nobody else in Oxford would have, either, even though it would change the course of their lives irreversibly.

My dad did well in school, but he wasn't a genius or even close to one. Not yet interested in girls, he was consumed by sports, where he excelled as a gifted athlete, quick and strong. His sport of choice was football. He began to play in junior high at Butner Stem, and it was a perfect outlet for his aggressive, competitive nature.

By the time he reached J. F. Webb high school, everybody knew who Jimmy Davis was. Outstanding in every aspect of the game, he became the football team's quarterback, which is arguably the most important and highest-profile position. Quickly, his prowess became known throughout North Carolina and beyond. During his junior year, he was so good that he was scouted by college recruiters far and wide, elevating his future prospects.

At the end of his very successful junior season, my father was offered a full scholarship to play football at Duke University. Even back in the 1930s, Duke was considered to be one of the best and most prestigious universities in the United States.

My father accepted the scholarship immediately. The future course of his life, which had no value or worth to my grandfather, skyrocketed. He was recognized and valued by others. By playing quarterback at Duke, his future would be set for life. He would become a man of stature in North Carolina and perhaps far beyond. Quarterbacks often are.

Needless to say, my dad was thrilled and grateful. He was looking forward to attending college and playing football for the Blue Devils. All that was required was for him was to finish high school. But, as it turned out, this illustrious future—becoming a football star at Duke—wasn't to be.

Instead, fate intervened disastrously. By the late winter of 1938, perhaps during the same week that the Anschluss occurred in Germany—which resulted in the incorporation of Austria into the Third Reich—the orphanage's administrator called my dad and his brother Frank into the office.

Looking at the boys with an unusual degree of concern, the administrator said, "I need to discuss something with the two of you. It's very important."

As serious as the man's voice was, my dad and Frank looked at each other. They wondered what kind of trouble they were in.

"What is it?" Frank asked.

Looking at the boys compassionately, the man said, "The two of you have been at the Masonic Home for quite a few years now." Sighing, he added, "I'm sorry to say, but it's time for you to move on. There are others, younger children, who need your beds."

"But we're allowed to stay until our nineteenth birthday," Frank countered.

"I know," the man admitted, "but we just can't afford to keep you. The Depression has put a tremendous strain on us."

"But we don't have any place to go!" Frank pleaded, adding, "What will we do?"

Shaken by this rebuttal, the man hardened. Becoming quite firm, he replied, "I'm not telling you to leave. I'm asking you to volunteer."

When the boys heard this, although they knew it wasn't really a request, they recognized that their time at the orphanage had come to an end. This meant they would soon be on their own. They would have to go to work to survive. It also meant that my dad wouldn't be able to graduate high school, the one requirement necessary to pursue his education and secure his football scholarship to Duke. His future in athletics had come to an end before it even began.

Now pushed out the door, my dad's prospects evaporated. There would be no bargaining with the orphanage's administrator, and continued complaining would be useless. He and Frank were cast aside so that other, younger kids could be allowed to enter. Although neither brother was prepared for this, like always, they looked to the future, not to the past.

Less than a week later, after saying goodbye to their younger brother and other friends at the orphanage, both Frank and my dad were walked to the front door by the administrator, each having been provided with a fresh pair of underwear and a crisp five-dollar bill. The man smiled, shook their hands, wished them well, and pointed to the world beyond, clearly implying it was theirs to conquer. Then, he shut the door behind them. They were now on their own.

Perseverance and persistence in spite of all
obstacles, discouragements, and impossibilities:
It is this, that in all things distinguishes
the strong soul from the weak.

THOMAS CARLYLE

Chapter 3

*** ★ ★ ★ ***

SPIT-SHINING SHOES

*Spectacular achievement is always preceded
by unspectacular preparation.*

—Robert S. Schuller

As my dad and Uncle Frank walked down the familiar streets of Oxford, they kept looking at their five-dollar bills. Neither had ever seen or had that much money before, not in their entire lives. It made both of them smile and joke about being rich, but they knew they weren't.

It was rare for them to have any money at all. From time to time, they might earn pocket change but, living at the orphanage, they were nearly always penniless. If they did perform an odd job, it was doing something that nobody else wanted to do or was incapable of doing, like shoveling a driveway after a snowstorm. They were lucky if they got paid a quarter for such tasks. Despite now having ten dollars between them, which would be the equivalent of $216 in today's economy, both realized that it wouldn't last very long.

That meant they needed to find work—and fast. Seeking employment, they visited every place in town they could think of, which didn't take long, not in a town with fewer than four thousand people. Unfortunately, neither could find anything. There simply wasn't any work to be had.

Sleeping outside or in an empty barn to be as frugal as possible, they quickly realized they wouldn't be able to survive in such a small town. Having already spent more than one dollar each on food, Frank decided that they needed to move to a bigger city, to a place where employment opportunities would be more readily available.

After agreeing that this was prudent, instead of taking a Trailways bus, they saved money by hitchhiking to the largest city they knew—Raleigh, North Carolina. With both boys having been born on Hanging Dog Mountain and raised in Oxford, moving to a town the size of Raleigh, which was about forty-eight thousand before the war, seemed like it was Metropolis to them.

Located just forty miles south of Oxford, it wasn't far from everything they knew. As close as they were, they would be able to hitchhike back to the orphanage to see their younger brother. This was a commitment both Frank and my dad made. Leaving Robert behind, which they were forced to do, was the most difficult thing either had ever done.

The morning Frank and my dad left the orphanage, Robert was nearly inconsolable. Feeling particularly alone after being separated from his brothers, he was grief-stricken. Recognizing this, both Frank and my dad promised to return for visits and not abandon him.

They didn't tell Robert they were leaving Oxford, though. As young as Robert was, that would have been too much for him to bear. Besides, returning to the orphanage so soon after being cast out didn't seem like a good idea.

Both Frank and my dad were well known to everybody in their small town, especially my dad, since he was the star of the high school football team, so catching a ride to Raleigh wasn't difficult. Besides, North Carolina's capital was just forty miles south—a straight shot down Highway 50.

Arriving in the big city, the pair set out to find employment. With their funds dwindling fast, they had to find work, but it wasn't easy. Jobs were scarce in 1938. The Great Depression had taken a devastating financial toll on the nation, but my dad and Frank were young, strong, energetic, and determined.

Despite this, their irresistible force of optimism came crashing down against the immovable object of universal poverty. Because want and scarcity were ubiquitous, nobody was hiring. They looked everywhere but with no luck.

Their situation became desperate. They were used to adhering to a regimented lifestyle at the orphanage, and as young as they were, it was difficult to adjust to not having any accountability or boundaries. Although they had never been this free before, their only goal was to survive.

With no foreseeable employment looming after a week of fruitless job hunting, Frank made a strategic decision. He walked into the US Army recruiting station and enlisted right on the spot. Being shipped out almost immediately to Fort Dix, New Jersey, his future was set for the next three years. At least he would be housed and fed.

Giving my dad what remained of his five dollars, Frank boarded a bus paid for by the army and headed north. Frank's situation was resolved. This relieved him immensely, but it made my dad's dilemma even more precarious. He was all alone in an unfamiliar city. Just seventeen and nearly broke, with no job and no prospects, the pressure on him must have been overwhelming.

He couldn't follow in Frank's footsteps either. The army required a young man to be eighteen before enlisting. This meant my dad wouldn't be eligible for another year.

Before leaving, Frank promised to send his brother whatever he could to help out but, being paid less than one thousand dollars per year, there would never be enough to fulfill his pledge.

My dad was on his own, which he understood and felt down to the molecular level of his existence. Two weeks earlier, while still living at the orphanage, with a football scholarship secured to attend Duke, my dad's future seemed very promising. Now, just a fortnight later, his prospects had deteriorated dramatically.

Frank was gone. In his absence, my dad was completely alone, jobless and homeless, without even a small measure of family support. Such a predicament might have been enough to bring even the most optimistic person to a grinding halt, but not my dad. Maintaining a positive attitude, he continued his search until he eventually found work as a cobbler's apprentice.

This is a vocation that has almost ceased to exist. Back then, however, during the Depression, when people's shoes wore out, they didn't have the luxury of buying new ones. Instead, when they could no longer wear their shoes, most would take them to a cobbler to be reheeled and resoled. This saved a substantial amount of money. To make the shoes look as new as possible, which pleased the customers when they picked them up, the shoes were always shined. This was my father's job.

Making old shoes look new was the only employment my dad could find, but it was a job. He was grateful to spit-shine shoes for people who were so poor that they couldn't afford to buy new ones. Although this was obviously a menial task, it was work, and my dad was thankful to have secured it. Choosing gratitude over resentment, which is the position of winners, he made the most of his difficult situation.

He must have smiled at the irony, though. Along with being qualified to run the offense for Duke University's Blue Devil football team, which was obviously prestigious, Jimmy Davis only seemed to be qualified for shining shoes, which wasn't prestigious at all. Nevertheless, just like he always did, he worked his tail off. Along with sweeping out the store and running errands for the store's owner, my dad shined shoes all day long. He earned as much as fifteen cents for each pair. It wasn't much, but it was honest work.

Shining shoes paid my dad enough to rent a room, which had access to a bathroom. He also had enough funds to buy food. This was a meager existence by any standard, and as a high school dropout, my dad had a future that no longer appeared to be bright. Nevertheless, having a job, even a menial one, meant that he would survive. He became quite proficient at shining shoes, but doing this wasn't much of a life.

At the rooming house, his accommodations were humid and hot, especially during the summer months. They were also poorly ventilated. With numerous vagrants occupying the other rooms, perhaps criminals as well, my dad always slept with one eye open. As young and fit as he was, he never had a problem, though. People knew not to mess with him. Besides, it was obvious he didn't have anything worth stealing.

While all of this was occurring in Raleigh, Jimmy's brother had just finished basic training at Fort Dix. Having been given his orders, he was stationed at Fort Bragg in North Carolina. In a letter Frank sent to my dad, he said that he was glad to be in the army. Enlisting had been a wise decision. The words "a wise decision" stuck in my dad's mind.

Rereading Frank's letter numerous times set my dad to thinking. Tired of shining smelly old shoes for people while living in a one-room apartment that was even smellier, and knowing there would never be a future in what he was doing, my dad made his own strategic decision.

One afternoon, he walked into the army recruiting center, the same one his brother had entered months earlier. Stepping up to the desk, speaking to the officer in charge, my dad said, "Sir, I want to enlist."

"Do you really?" the officer replied.

"Yes, sir."

"How old are you, son?" the officer inquired.

Without hesitation, my dad replied, "Eighteen, sir."

"Are you sure you're eighteen?" the recruiting officer asked skeptically.

"Yes, sir," my dad replied, lying with a straight face, affirming that he was old enough to enlist.

Before the war, but especially after it began, it was quite common for seventeen-year-olds to lie about their age. Needing young, fit soldiers, it was equally as common for recruiting officers to take these kids at their word. The reason was obvious. Events were transpiring in Europe that required the United States to build a large, well-prepared armed forces.

That afternoon at the recruiting station, my dad wasn't even asked to produce a birth certificate. Even if he had been asked, he wouldn't have been able to. If one existed, the only person who would have had access to it was his father—a man my dad hadn't seen or spoken to in more than a decade.

So, asking my father about his age was more of a formality than anything else. Although he still didn't need to shave—he was strong, muscular, and fit from having trained to play football for years—he was precisely the type of enlistee the army was seeking.

Accepted immediately, Jimmy Davis was now a new recruit.

That afternoon, with a smile on his face, my dad gave notice to the cobbler, who was sorry to see him leave. Shining his last pair of shoes a few days later, Jimmy boarded the same bus his brother had several months earlier. It was headed to the same location—Fort Dix, New Jersey. This was where he began his basic training as a buck private. I knew it was Fort Dix from conversations my dad had with me years later.

While my dad was being trained for future duty, in Germany earth-shattering events were transpiring at record speed. During the exact timeframe when my dad enlisted, Britain's prime minister, Neville Chamberlain, forged an agreement with Adolf Hitler. Known as the Munich Agreement, the treaty permitted the Sudetenland of Czechoslovakia to be taken from the Czechs and incorporated into the German Reich.

Returning to England with a smile on his face and an umbrella in his hand, Chamberlain announced to the British people and the rest of the world that he had secured "peace in our time." Eager for this to be true, the Brits felt a sense of relief. In the USA, most people viewed these events the same way. Wanting peace and wishing not to be entangled in the sordid affairs of Europe, Americans desired more than anything to be left alone. Trying to weather the Great Depression was enough stress for them to face.

Little did any who lived in either English-speaking country realize it, but the Munich Agreement meant that Hitler had put nearly the last piece of the puzzle in place, ensuring that World War II would be inevitable. Most of the world wouldn't be prepared for what was about to occur, but after completing basic training, my father certainly was.

Every event Jimmy Davis had ever experienced, every disappointment he had ever suffered, every deprivation he had ever endured, would prove to be absolutely necessity. It would help him survive the most bloody, destructive, and violent war of all time, World War II. In life, we generally learn by looking back. It's where we gain most of our wisdom.

Although oblivious to any of this, as almost any seventeen-year-old would be, my father was well suited for the task that lay before him. As an integral part of the Greatest Generation, destiny awaited him. Without ever having heard the term, let alone understand what it meant, along with five million others, Jimmy Davis was about to become an irreplaceable, glorious part of American history.

If you're a true warrior, competition doesn't scare you. It makes you better.

ANDREW WHITWORTH

Chapter 4

★ ★ ★

DRAWN INTO THE CONFLICT

*The object of war is not to die for your country
but to make the other bastard die for his.*

—George S. Patton

Before shipping out, Jimmy Davis hitchhiked back to Oxford to say goodbye to his brother Robert, telling him that he would write him weekly. This was a promise my dad kept, except for when he was going through boot camp, when it wasn't allowed. Frank Davis did the same. Unlike his two older brothers, Robert was allowed to remain at the orphanage until his nineteenth birthday. All three of Edgar's sons were pleased about that. Resilient, like his older brothers, Robert thrived in Oxford.

Upon completing his basic training in late 1938 or early 1939, my father was shipped south to be stationed at Fort Benning in Columbus, Georgia. War had not yet begun in Europe, but hostilities seemed inevitable. Becoming embroiled in the affairs of Europe wasn't what the average American citizen desired. Wanting to remain neutral, a majority of Americans were quite vocal about their opposition to any conflict.

Knowing this, but certain that war would eventuate and equally certain that the USA would be drawn into the conflict, the army faced a Herculean task. It was required to do its best to be prepared for the worst and to make each young recruit battle-worthy. My dad was among those recruits.

Always diligent, Jimmy Davis trained hard, never becoming complacent about what was required of him. Being in shape came naturally to him. With his football career cut short, as competitive as he was, he took up another contact sport on the base: boxing.

At all military bases before the war, whether in the army, navy, or marines, boxing matches were held regularly, pitting one soldier against another. This brutal sport was right up my father's alley. He loved it. In precisely the same way he'd become an exceptional quarterback, he became an accomplished pugilist as well.

I can't accentuate enough what a huge sport boxing was back then. It was so popular that young soldiers lined up to watch every fight. Bouts were the most popular events on base. Not surprisingly, soldiers liked to bet on who would win. Although it was forbidden by the army, most officers looked the other way. Betting occurred all the time.

Money wasn't the only currency used to gamble. If a young soldier didn't have any money, which was frequently the case, he would bet his cigarette allotment. During this period everybody smoked, including my father. Like most of the other soldiers, the military was where he picked up the habit. The army provided Camels and Lucky Strikes to the soldiers. With filtered cigarettes not yet having been invented, "smokes" became a second medium of exchange.

This lasted throughout the war, both at home and abroad, and during the period of reconstruction after the war. Bartered regularly, a pack of American cigarettes was a valuable commodity, as were Hershey's chocolate bars, which were also provided to the troops. Both could get a soldier a free meal, perhaps something even more than that from a woman.

Like everything else Jimmy Davis chose to pursue, he became a proficient boxer. A hard puncher, he was fearless and could take a punch. Never retreating in the ring, he became the welterweight champion on his base. This accomplishment gained him substantial notoriety and respect among the troops.

Nobody messed with my dad, that's for sure, not if they knew what was good for them. Those who knew him well never bet against him either. Winning them money and cigarettes consistently, Jimmy rarely let his bettors down.

Life in the army was regimented, even more so than it is today. Adjusting to this Spartan lifestyle was difficult for many of the young soldiers, but not for my father. In many ways, it wasn't much different than what he experienced growing up at the orphanage. Sleeping in the barracks with so many other men was similar to sleeping in his dormitory in Oxford. Going through a line in the mess hall to be served breakfast, lunch, and dinner was precisely the same routine that occurred at the orphanage. Because of these similarities, my father thrived in the military.

When the war broke out, which occurred when the Nazis invaded Poland on September 6, 1939, the world was shocked, but it shouldn't have been. War had been inevitable for years. That September day in Columbus, Georgia, it was hot and sticky. Early Septembers in the deep South are often sweltering. Hearing the news, although the USA was not directly involved—not yet—everybody at Fort Benning had a foreboding sense about what the future would hold.

Those who had already tasted battle became subdued, knowing what war was really like. Those who had never experienced it, the young and naïve, displayed a measure of bravado. Such a reaction is typical for young soldiers, most of whom were still teenagers. Never having served in combat, they were eager to become involved. At least, that was the initial reaction many had.

The response from the American people was substantially different, especially among those who had fought in the Great War two decades earlier—the war which came to be known as World War I. Having experienced so much carnage, they didn't want any part of a second helping.

Despite the overwhelming desire of most Americans to refrain from participating in a European war, the army had no choice but to prepare for what might eventuate. This included keeping seasoned soldiers in uniform, including my father, and Uncle Frank too.

My father's three-year enlistment ended in 1940, more than a full year before the USA entered the Second World War. Yet he was certain that the nation would somehow be drawn into the conflict, so declining to reenlist was never a consideration for my dad. Serving his country was Jimmy Davis's responsibility. Intuitively, he understood this.

He knew that the responsibility for protecting our country was his duty. No alternative perspective entered his mind, nor did it for millions of his peers. Being this resolute and selfless was what made them the Greatest Generation—a venerated title they will never lose. I cannot tell you how proud it makes me to have been the direct beneficiary of the sacrifices they made.

Although just twenty years old, because he'd lied about his age to join, Jimmy was already an experienced soldier. Knowing his country needed him, there was no way he would consider walking away. He wasn't like that, nor were any of his comrades in arms. He probably would have been drafted back in anyway, but there was no need for that, not where Jimmy Davis was concerned.

Like a true Tennessean, this man who was born just a few miles east of that great state on Hanging Dog Mountain volunteered. Besides, he certainly didn't want to go back to the rank of buck private. Already a corporal by that time, he had achieved a measure of success that made him feel important, perhaps for the first time in his life, other than when he received the Duke scholarship.

★ ★ ★

When I was young, beginning at the age of seven or eight, just before the time when John F. Kennedy was elected to be the first Catholic president, stories about what had happened during the war fascinated me. Like all boys my age, I was eager to learn about what my dad did during World War II, what battles he fought in, how much action he saw, and if he ever shot anyone. I wanted my dad to tell me everything about his time in the army, leaving nothing out.

I asked him about the war many times, badgering him, but he was equally as hesitant to discuss his experiences. His response, or more accurately his lack of a response, wasn't uncommon for veterans. Men who fought the Nazis, ultimately defeating them soundly, were often reticent to divulge their experiences.

Because my dad was committed to not talking about it, some of what I know concerning his role in the war is sketchy. What I do know is that the part he played was clearly significant.

When war broke out for the USA, which began when the Empire of Japan attacked Pearl Harbor on December 7, 1941—a "date which will live in infamy," according to President Franklin D. Roosevelt—a huge military buildup began throughout the nation. The war effort consumed everything. It was so extensive that neither Ford, Chrysler, nor General Motors produced even one domestic automobile throughout the duration of the war. Instead, they retooled their manufacturing plants to produce tanks, armored vehicles, jeeps, and trucks, enough weaponry to outfit the USA, Great Britain, and the Soviet Union.

Even before the war began, President Roosevelt, feeling certain that US involvement in it would be inevitable, met with British Prime Minister Winston Churchill in Newfoundland. This was when they determined that the defeat of Nazi Germany would be the primary focus of the war, allowing no other purpose to supersede it, but that's not all. They also agreed that they would accept nothing less than total surrender. Knowing that Hitler would use a ceasefire to rearm, no negotiated peace with the Nazis would be permitted. Having made this decision, even the attack by the Japanese less than six months later didn't deter the Allies from their primary objective, destroying Hitler.

Known as the Atlantic Charter, the joint declaration created at this rendezvous impacted my father, his platoon, and everybody stationed at Fort Benning. It meant that when America did enter the war, my dad would be sent to Europe to fight, not to the Pacific.

A sergeant by the time hostilities broke out involving the USA, my dad remained at Fort Benning. Eventually, he was sent to England to train and prepare for the invasion of Europe. The buildup of American soldiers abroad was extensive. Hundreds of thousands of GIs were stationed at numerous bases scattered across England. They were there for a substantial amount of time, some for more than a year before the Normandy invasion.

While on leave, my dad and his buddies never hung around the base. Frequently, they would take the ferry over to Ireland, where they would drink beer that was colored green, laugh, carouse, and generally make a nuisance of themselves—all in good fun, of course.

Being pent up and anticipating the inevitable battles was difficult for these young men. They wanted to get on with it while simultaneously dreading what might happen. While desiring to put their training to use, they also feared what the consequences might be. This dichotomy produced apprehension that required an outlet.

Not surprisingly, their leaves and furloughs produced some wild times. With many of the British soldiers already fighting in North Africa, the lassies left behind were thrilled to have so many Yanks available to take their place. Most of the British people, especially the older ones, weren't nearly as thrilled to have so many American soldiers around. Concerning their presence, the Brits routinely described our troops as "overpaid, oversexed, and over here."

I wanted my dad to tell me about those adventures as well, but he never did. When I tried to coax him to be candid, he would smile, but he refrained from being as forthcoming as I hoped. Nevertheless, I did notice that he always had a mischievous glint in his eye and a slight smile on his face when I brought up the subject. This allowed me to put two and two together, which I loved to do, even though I never knew many of the specifics.

Obviously, he didn't like to kiss and tell. Thinking about his adventures all these decades later still makes me smile. What a time they must have had.

The closer they came to being cast into battle, the harder they partied on Saturday nights, but on Sunday mornings the number of soldiers attending worship services also grew exponentially. Many were fearful they would meet their Maker soon. Having almost no religious background, my dad began to wear a Saint Christopher medallion around his neck. Knowing that there were no atheists in foxholes, my father took his first foray into faith, but it would not be his last one.

* * *

My father didn't storm the beaches of Normandy on June 6, 1944, like many of the other soldiers stationed in England. None of the men at his base did either. Although this was frustrating, and not to their liking, they had no idea what awaited them. On D-Day, instead of engaging in the battle, like everybody else throughout the world, my dad and his friends were glued to the radio. They anxiously listened to all of the news about what was happening on the coast of France.

Instead of being included in the initial assault, my dad's battalion, which was under the command of General George S. Patton, was held back. Patton's men, including my father, constituted the newly formed Third Army. They were reserved for another purpose. Even though they had no idea what that purpose would be and were never informed or consulted, they knew it was destined to be significant. This realization was based on the intensity of the training that followed the initial landing. Under the command of the USA's best general, they felt certain they wouldn't be held back for long.

The weeks that followed D-Day were equally as intense as what they'd experienced in basic training. The effort forged this group of men, a large number of whom were inexperienced, into a first-rate fighting machine. Based on these factors, my dad and his friends came to recognize the importance of what awaited them.

In the evenings, after an intense day of training, my dad and his best friend, Billy Winthrop, wondered where they would be sent, what they would be tasked to do, and how dangerous it would be. That's all their discussions were, though—conjecture. Their prognostications were speculative. They didn't have a clue about what their future would entail, but they would soon find out.

On August 1, the entire Third Army, consisting of four army corps, deployed across the English Channel. Once on French soil, they engaged the enemy almost immediately, forcing the Germans to withdraw. Once this happened, the invasion, which had begun seven weeks earlier but had not yet achieved victory, finally was successful.

Until the Third Army arrived, the Allied foothold in France remained tenuous. Although German resistance was fierce, with the addition of Patton's Third Army, Allied victory was assured. The threat of the Allies being pushed out of France ceased.

Pursuing the retreating Germans across France after taking Avranches, followed by fierce fighting in the Falaise Pocket, victorious in each case, Patton's army moved at lightning speed all the way to Moselle within a month. Taking 94,000 German prisoners in the process, they finally ran out of gasoline, forcing them to stop and resupply.

As a squad leader, my dad was experiencing battle conditions in earnest. Once refueled, the Third Army broke loose and raced across France all the way to the Rhine River. They received accolades worldwide for their heroics, which pleased General Patton. Relentlessly pressing forward, Patton kept the Wehrmacht on its heels, winning battle after battle against the Germans, driving them out of France. Patton's pursuit was so fierce that the press referred to him as "General Blood and Guts." The soldiers serving under him amplified this moniker, declaring that it was *his* guts but *their* blood.

They engaged the enemy virtually nonstop. Summer turned into fall, with fall turning into winter. The Allies, having achieved continuous success since securing Normandy, felt certain victory was inevitable. Becoming somewhat complacent, they were surprised and unprepared for the counteroffensive launched by the Wehrmacht through the Ardennes Forest just before Christmas in 1944. At first quite successful, the Allied efforts to stop the advance stalled, resulting in the Battle of the Bulge.

For American troops, including my father, this was the largest and bloodiest battle of World War II. More than that, it was the third-largest battle in American history. It was so significant that the outcome of the war depended on winning it.

At Bastogne, the German advance was challenged by the 101st Airborne. The Americans were holding the town by a fingernail, but they were nearly out of food and ammunition. Unless help arrived soon, they wouldn't be able to survive.

To come to their aid, General Patton committed the Third Army.

Although my dad was always hesitant to discuss the war, he did tell me that he fought in the Battle of the Bulge. With this mêlée as famous as it was, it's only natural that I would press him for details. As insistent as I was, he finally capitulated one day.

With a trembling voice, he told me about what happened to Billy Winthrop, his best friend. Their unit had been trying to take out a German machine gun nest in the Ardennes, but the enemy was resisting stubbornly. While Billy was running from one position to another, a .30 caliber machine gun cut him in two, severing his body completely just above the waist.

In horror, my dad witnessed his best friend violently gunned down. He added, "The most difficult thing about it was Billy's legs didn't know he was dead yet. So, they just kept on running for another twenty feet. That was tough to see."

When I heard this, I finally understood why my father was so reluctant to talk about the war. The image of his best friend being cut in two was something he would see in his mind's eye for the rest of his life. It never left him. How could it? How could that image and the horror of what it depicted not affect him?

In the South, we have a saying about someone who doesn't know what they are doing. The aphorism states, "That guy's running around like a chicken with its head cut off." Folks below the Mason-Dixon Line, especially in rural areas, understand exactly what this means.

After that, when my dad thought about Billy, I'm sure he wanted to remember him as he had been—a smiling, funny, happy-go-lucky guy who was committed to doing his part in the war. I'm also sure that my dad never forgot seeing his best friend ripped apart by machine-gun fire.

What my dad witnessed was no different than what other veterans have witnessed and experienced. War is horrendous. Many of the soldiers faced similar things daily, but they knew how important winning was. That's why they didn't allow shocks like what happened to Billy Winthrop deter them.

Like so many GIs with the same motivation, the same commitment, my father fought the war so that my sisters and me—even though Jimmy Davis wasn't certain we would ever exist—would be free. He wanted the lives of those who would follow him to be better than his had been.

As I reflect upon his service, this is what spurred him on to sacrifice, not any nonsensical notion of white privilege. His determination was so strong that not even the fear of death deterred him. Thinking about it, I still marvel at such heroism.

After I heard the story about Billy Winthrop, I was never as invasive as I had previously been. Intuitively, I knew to be more circumspect, to be more careful and respectful about his privacy. I'm sure I wasn't perfect— kids never are—but I didn't want my father to experience any additional emotional pain just to satisfy my curiosity.

Obviously, the Battle of the Bulge was a great American victory, leading to the unconditional surrender of the Nazis less than six months later. Fighting in the snow, in the bitter cold, without hot food or a warm bed, enduring hardship for days, with the only warmth coming from mortars and grenades intended to kill them, these brave men accomplished more than they ever dreamed possible. Many died; many more were wounded.

The attrition rate was so high that my father received a field commission. He became a second lieutenant. Having been a high school dropout, he was proud to finish the war as an officer. I've always been proud of him for that as well.

Smiling, with a wink, Second Lieutenant Jimmy Davis would add, "It beat shinin' shoes."

> *Courage, above all things, is the*
> *first quality of a warrior.*
> CARL VON CLAUSEWITZ

Chapter 5

★ ★ ★

HAPPY DAYS ARE
HERE AGAIN

Dancing is a perpendicular expression
of a horizontal desire.
—George Bernard Shaw

With the German defeat at Bastogne, the key conflict in the Battle of the Bulge, the last offensive of the Third Reich ended badly. Less than five months later, Hitler was dead and Germany surrendered unconditionally. On May 7, 1945, the war in Europe concluded. Known as V-E Day, Victory in Europe, celebrations ensued across the continent and at home in the USA.

By that time, my father had fought in France, Germany, Austria, and Czechoslovakia. Battle-weary, like every other GI, Second Lieutenant Jimmy Davis was anxious to get on with his life. So were his two brothers, Frank and Robert. Fortunately, all three of May Bell Davis's sons survived the war. Many families weren't nearly as fortunate.

Having put their lives on hold for many years, nearly every GI in Europe was ready to go home, whether they'd volunteered or been drafted. With many committed to remain in uniform for the duration of the war plus six months, all that remained for the Second World War to conclude was the surrender of Japan. To accomplish this necessitated the invasion of the Japanese mainland, where nearly half a million American casualties were anticipated, with as many as a million wounded. Nobody looked forward to this daunting task. It would necessitate that the troops from Europe be shipped to the Pacific.

Although scheduled, this never happened. When the atomic bomb was dropped on Hiroshima and the hydrogen bomb dropped on Nagasaki, obliterating both cities, hostilities ended abruptly. Knowing that half a million American soldiers would survive because of the bomb— perhaps my dad among them—the American people were jubilant and grateful.

The Empire of Japan surrendered on August 15, 1945. Known as V-J Day, Victory over Japan, this concluded World War II. Invading Japan would no longer be required. All plans to ship additional troops to Asia were scrapped. This meant that most of the remaining American forces in Europe would be going home.

Because the Nazis surrendered in May, and Japan in August, this meant that several million GIs would arrive back in the States in time for Christmas. President Harry

S. Truman, who had succeeded FDR, was committed to making certain this happened. War-weary Americans, including those who anxiously awaited the return of their sons and the sweethearts of GIs, demanded this from the president. Wisely, Truman delivered.

Having put their lives on hold for years to make certain the United States would survive and never be enslaved by the Nazis or the Japanese, millions of healthy young men defeated both totalitarian regimes. These men were now ready to resume normal lives. Returning home, a large number married and started families immediately. Millions of babies were born in 1946 and the subsequent years. These children, known as baby boomers, were the immediate descendants of the Greatest Generation.

Interestingly, those who fought to defeat the Axis powers didn't seem to suffer from post-traumatic stress disorder, certainly not as significantly as more recent generations. I've always wondered about this. Although I'm not a psychiatrist, I have a theory.

I believe it's because World War II vets knew what they were fighting for. They had a single-minded purpose—one they knew, understood, and made a commitment to achieve without reservation. It was the survival of the United States and of the American way of life. They believed in their cause and in the war effort. Consequently, despite every hardship, they were determined to see it through until total victory could be achieved.

American soldiers since then have not had that same mindset, through no fault of their own. It's because they have been deployed for limited engagements by politicians, where victory has never been the end goal. Often, the purpose has remained undefined. Wars have been waged with purposes the average soldier doesn't understand, not like the Greatest Generation did. Consequently, the stress from fighting in seemingly purposeless, unwinnable encounters cost soldiers far more psychologically than it ever did World War II veterans.

With hostilities over, even though most troops returned to the USA, not all were this fortunate. My father was one of those who remained. Europe was in shambles. With people displaced, homeless, jobless, and without adequate provisions, coupled with increasing tensions with the Soviet Union, a large peacekeeping force was required to remain in Germany, Italy, and Great Britain.

This included my father. Stationed in Germany, he didn't return home in time for Christmas, nor in time for the following Christmas. In fact, he didn't return to the USA until late 1947 or early 1948.

By the time he was allowed to return, nearly all of his friends, as well as those who'd served in his platoon, were married. Many were already fathers. My dad wasn't, but he wanted to be. I believe this was the motivation that drove him forward, providing the hope and purpose he needed to survive the war.

When he enlisted in 1938, he did so believing that he would be out of the army shortly before his twenty-first birthday. Obviously, this isn't what happened. By the time he was discharged, he was already twenty-seven years old, maybe twenty-eight.

He missed all of the experiences of being a young man, including dating. During the entire period of his enlistment, he never had a girlfriend. Young, handsome, funny, and with money in his pocket, he had plenty of experiences with women, but that's all they were—experiences. He never developed a relationship, not with any of them. Like many GIs, he had sexual encounters, but he never had an attachment with a woman where a deep connection could be established, where a loving, mutually fulfilling relationship would flourish.

This stunted his development somewhat. Nearly all men realize they don't understand women as well as they should, but in my father's case, he was even more of a novice than most. Not only was he clueless about what made women tick, but his choosing mechanism was altered because of his lack of experience.

He didn't have the foggiest idea about what women were really like. This wasn't his fault, though. He'd never had the opportunity to interact with potential mates in a normal way. Based on his circumstances—growing up in an orphanage, shining shoes, and then fighting in a war for years—there was no opportunity for a young woman to be in his life.

Most young men choose women based on similarities to their mothers, but of course, Jimmy's mom had died before he was six years old. Although he loved and revered her, May Bell Davis never had the molding influence that her young son required. She wasn't there to direct him, correct him, or help him develop his character. She wasn't available to teach, nurture, or guide him. As a result, my dad didn't know what to look for and what to avoid.

Dad would have to learn on his own. Because of the war, he wasn't even able to do this adequately. Carousing weekend romances were all he had ever experienced. This meant he knew women physically but not emotionally. This affected his ability to choose a woman wisely.

Kids whose moms are alcoholics have the same problem. Their modeling becomes twisted. Because of this, they make poor choices, not realizing it until it's too late.

My dad certainly didn't receive any maternal direction at the orphanage either. Although he was cared for by women, they were employed to cook his meals and maintain the large facility. That's all. They liked Jimmy—everybody did—but none of his caretakers loved him, not like his mother would have had she survived.

This meant that when my father began to look for a mate, he didn't have the slightest idea about what he was doing. Despite this, he knew his end goal: he wanted a family—a family much different than his had been. To achieve his goal required meeting a potential wife. He was committed to finding a good one. Now in his late twenties, he thought this would be an easy task.

He wanted to have a good marriage, but he was even more committed to being a great father. The one thing he knew for certain was that he never wanted to be like his dad.

With Jimmy's paternal modeling having been abysmal, he already had an abundance of wisdom about what he didn't want to be like. To him, being a good father was the antithesis of Edgar Davis—a complete failure who abandoned his children. Since Edgar never loved his children, at the core of my father's being, he was committed to becoming the best dad he could possibly be. Knowing he could achieve this goal, he dedicated himself to it, years before any of his four children were born. I can assure you that this was a commitment he kept.

To find a woman, Jimmy did exactly what he had been doing during his years in the army. He looked for the prettiest girl he could find, one who was a good dancer. This was the entirety of what he required. Although his strategy was naïve and simplistic, this was how he went about seeking a wife. As inexperienced as he was about what women are really like, what he was doing seemed normal to him. During his entire time in Europe, other than how to survive, these were the thoughts that dominated his mind.

His strategy wasn't unique. Many others pursued the same unrealistic pattern, expecting it to succeed. Men are like that; women are not. Like my dad, other soldiers went about finding a wife in precisely the same manner.

This strategy is one that has transcended the ages. Two millennia ago, the Roman emperor Marcus Aurelius made this observation: "The art of living is more like wrestling than dancing."

Nothing defines humans better than their
willingness to do irrational things
in the pursuit of phenomenally unlikely payoffs.
This is the principle behind lotteries and dating.

SCOTT ADAMS

Chapter 6

* * *

THE RED CLAY OF
THE DEEP SOUTH

It is well that war is so terrible,
otherwise we should grow too fond of it.
—ROBERT E. LEE

The final two battles my father fought in World War II involved the liberation of Austria and Czechoslovakia. When the war concluded, having traipsed across Europe with Patton's Third Army, mostly by foot, Jimmy Davis ended up in Prague. With the cessation of hostilities, he was assigned to serve in Germany. Returning there, he became part of the US peacekeeping force. This was where he witnessed Nazi atrocities firsthand.

He was at the death camps, not after they had been preserved as sanitized historical monuments of the Third

Reich's war crimes, not when they were places for future generations to visit, but when the few surviving prisoners were present. Skeletal, too frail to be moved, these surviving Jews had to be fed a special diet simply to survive. What they ate contained steroids, the kind that future athletes would use illegally to enhance their performance. For the death camp survivors, these supplements helped build back their depleted muscle mass quickly. Even so, many were so weak they didn't survive.

Witnessing this was difficult for all the GIs. The horror they saw affected them for years. The concentration camps were a grim reminder of precisely how evil the Nazis were.

It wasn't just what they saw with their eyes that was difficult. It was the smell of the camps as well. The stench of death permeated everything. The odors of putrescine and cadaverine were omnipresent, lingering in the air, remaining months after the murders and cremations had ceased. This foulness was something my dad would never forget.

With the collapse of the Third Reich, where rigid conformity to the regime's policies was strictly enforced, an era of lawlessness swept over war-torn Europe. With the economies of each European nation devastated, and some countries practically ceasing to exist, American soldiers were required to maintain the peace. This was particularly true in western Germany, where law and order resembled the Old West. The only sense of stability came from the presence of American GIs and British Tommies.

In eastern Germany, which was occupied by the Soviets, the Russians were more interested in exacting retribution on the German people than in helping them to restore order. Almost immediately, tensions escalated between the two sides of the nation, which would officially become East Germany and West Germany on October 7, 1949. Some feared conflict between the Soviets and the Americans would ensue. Thankfully, it didn't.

Other potential powder kegs developed as well. Maintaining peace during the Nuremberg Trials, the event where Nazi war criminals were held accountable for their death camp atrocities, became a challenge. Most wanted to hang the Nazis, while others lobbied on their behalf, demanding that they receive no punishment at all.

This was a difficult time for nearly every GI, including my father. There were constant threats of violence. Despite the war having ended, because a prolonged, hostile environment continued, American soldiers became de facto policemen. Their presence was absolutely required.

By this time in my father's life, although still a young man by today's standards, just twenty-seven or twenty-eight, he had seen more death and carnage than a dozen combined would see in their entire lifetimes. Constantly surrounded by so much evil over such an extended period of time, and receiving no respite from it, my dad had no trouble believing there was a Devil. He had been rubbing shoulders with him and the forces of evil for years.

My dad reasoned that if Satan did exist, which he was certain was the case, a benevolent God must also exist. You couldn't have one without the other.

As noted earlier, while preparing for battle in 1944, my dad had contemplated the idea that there are no atheists in a foxhole. Almost to a man, World War II veterans would agree that this was true. My father certainly would have, but he also recognized that there was a significant void in his life. He lacked a meaningful spiritual dimension.

My dad had been trained to kill, but he had never received any formal training in matters of faith. This created a deep emptiness within him. Although he wore a Saint Christopher medallion, all it represented was a charm. Like a talisman, he had come to depend on it, but he didn't have a clue about who Saint Christopher was.

Having tasted battle nonstop since the day he landed in France until the day the Nazis finally surrendered, whenever he was in a tight situation—like the Ardennes Forest, the place where his best friend was gunned down—my father prayed to God. Asking to be spared, to be protected, my dad begged God to provide him with the strength to carry on. To Jimmy Davis, God had become very real, but who the Almighty really was had never been clearly defined to him.

Like so many other GIs, my dad committed his life to serve God if he was spared, but he had no idea what that would look like. To Jimmy, it was just an amorphous idea, a loose concept. At the same time, he knew it was absolutely real. Although this was a commitment many abandoned completely after the war, my dad never did. It became part of who he was. Although it was still dormant, his faith was waiting to burst forth.

★ ★ ★

By the time global hostilities ceased in the summer of 1945, there were eight million Americans, mostly men but some women, scattered across the globe in uniform. The greatest number were in Europe, five million, but there were another three million throughout the Pacific, Asia, and North Africa. Bringing the troops home, which became known as Operation Magic Carpet, became an all-consuming project. It was a Herculean effort, requiring hundreds of ships to make numerous trips across the ocean.

Unfortunately, my father wasn't part of this operation. He wasn't allowed to be repatriated in 1945. When his orders finally came through more than two years later, allowing him to return to the States for the first time since being deployed before the Normandy invasion, he was ecstatic. Overjoyed, he read his orders over and over, just to make certain that going home was really in the cards for him.

By the time he finally left Europe, Operation Magic Carpet, an extraordinary success, had long since terminated. Despite this, my dad returned home on the *RMS Queen Mary*, along with several thousand other GIs.

After taking nearly a week to cross the Atlantic, the ship entered New York Harbor and sailed past the Statue of Liberty. Everybody onboard, including my dad, wept with joy to be alive and to be returning to the USA. This patriotic occasion was one of the most inspiring moments of my father's life.

This is one part of his military service that he recounted often. Like him, it made me proud to be an American.

Unlike some in the younger generations, I've never lost my love for being an American. It's hardwired into my DNA.

Disembarking from the ship, setting foot on American soil, and mustered out of the army a short time later, Jimmy was ready to move forward with his life. Even so, his return home was unlike most others'. He didn't have parents to greet him, nor a sweetheart to kiss him when he got off of the ship. Nobody was waiting for him.

Once again, just like when he was a shoeshine boy, he was all alone. He didn't even have a home to return to. Similar to the day when he was cut loose by the orphanage, Lieutenant Jimmy Davis was homeless.

His brothers, Frank and Robert (who eventually joined the war effort), had returned to the States a few years earlier. They were already married and had settled down. Both were working at the Pactiv Evergreen paper mill in Canton, North Carolina. They would remain employed there for the rest of their lives. With both having young families, neither had a spot in their home for their brother. Although the three kept in touch by mail, it was clear my uncles had found their place in the world, but my dad still hadn't.

Canton was just a hundred miles from where the siblings had been born on Hanging Dog Mountain, and my uncles loved returning to this mountainous area. Working their way up the ladder at the paper mill while raising their children and enjoying married life, both eventually became executives with well-paying jobs. Frank and Robert were happy and financially set for life.

Undeterred by having no prospects of his own, my father only had one housing option. It was with his crippled sister, Mary Jo. Having defied the odds, she not only had survived polio, but also thrived afterwards. Unable to use her legs, she became extraordinarily proficient at using her hands. Working at the Jewel Box in Cedartown, Georgia, she made jewelry, but that's not all she did. She also repaired watches—a tedious, difficult skill to master.

Mary Jo lived a quiet, tranquil life in a small rental house on the outskirts of town. When she learned about her older brother's plight, that he would be homeless upon his return, she reached out to him by mail, offering him a room.

Deciding to take up Mary Jo's offer, primarily because he didn't have any place else to go, Jimmy boarded a night train in Grand Central Station soon after landing, headed for Atlanta. Once he arrived in Georgia's capital, he planned to take the bus to Cedartown, which was located sixty miles northwest of Atlanta.

Once aboard the train, as tired as he was, my dad fell into a deep sleep. He didn't awaken until the following morning. As the train was passing through North Carolina, he looked out the window at the countryside. Seeing the red clay of the Deep South for the first time in years, he smiled, knowing he was finally home. This was where he belonged.

Jimmy Davis was a true Southerner and always would be. Just being in the South once again, he no longer felt alone. Rejuvenated, he couldn't wait to get started with the rest of his life. He lit a Camel and smoked it, smiling about the future.

This was the first thing he did every morning, even before he had his first cup of coffee. Oblivious to the long-term effects of smoking, just like nearly every other veteran of the war, he smoked a pack a day. Once he finished his cigarette, confident about the direction of his life, he found the dining car, had a cup of coffee, and then ate a hearty breakfast.

* * *

Arriving at Mary Jo's house late that evening after having spent the past twenty-four hours traveling, although he was exhausted, my dad was delighted to see his sister. She was equally thrilled. When Jimmy leaned down, she hugged him so long and so hard that he thought he would pull a muscle in his back, but he didn't care. He had a home and a place to stay, at least for a while. He wouldn't be content to be a boarder at his sister's house, though, at least not long-term.

He had waited years to begin his life and was more than anxious to get started. Although he wanted to find a woman, that would have to wait. If he wanted to eat regularly, which he did, he needed a job. In a town the size of Cedartown, with a population of slightly over 9,500 people, finding employment was going to be a challenge. Refusing to be dependent on his younger sister, he needed to overcome the obstacle of being unemployed quickly.

When Mary Jo informed her brother that there was an opening at the Jewel Box where she worked, Jimmy jumped at the opportunity. He applied the next day and was hired on the spot. Even though the job wasn't prestigious, my dad was grateful to have it.

Smart and engaging, he would be responsible for greeting customers and selling them jewelry, but that was just part of his job description. He would also be responsible for stocking the shelves, sweeping the floors, and even making the coffee. He would do all of this while his baby sister did the important work in the back of the store, creating new products.

Jimmy didn't mind. He was thankful to be employed. Not having a car meant he wouldn't have the opportunity to drive to Atlanta on his days off, so he wouldn't be able to meet any eligible women. He would have to put finding a girlfriend on the back burner. Although he didn't like this limitation, there was nothing he could do about it.

Settling in to his new way of life, which was far more sedentary than the adventurous life he'd led for so many years, he did what he always did. He made the best out of his situation.

In addition to working six days a week, he made plans to finish high school, but obtaining a general equivalency diploma (GED) wouldn't be enough, not for my dad. He intended to be the first person in his family to earn a college degree. This was a promise he made to himself, a commitment he intended to fulfill, but securing his GED had to come first—which he did, of course, accomplish.

One day several months later, when the store was empty, he began to look at a brochure from Berry College. It was located in nearby Rome, just twenty miles north. While my dad was busily engaged reading what the college had to offer, the door to the store opened, ringing a bell that announced a customer had entered.

Quickly putting his brochure under the counter, my dad looked up. What he witnessed stunned him so much that, for a brief moment, he was unable to speak. To his wonderment, the most beautiful woman he had ever seen walked into the store. He recovered quickly, welcoming her when she approached.

Coming straight to the point, the woman announced, "I'm looking for a pair of earrings. Can you help me?"

With the mischievous smile that his army buddies knew well, my dad replied, "I believe I can. In fact, I'm sure I can."

Love is not blind. Romance is.
Romance is the most dangerous thing.
Romance is like an illusion.
It shows you things, and you hear things that don't exist.
HRITHIK ROSHAN

Chapter 7

★ ★ ★

MARRIAGE MATERIAL

*Love is composed of a single soul
inhabiting two bodies.*

—Aristotle

The lovely young lady spent more than an hour at the Jewel Box, trying on nearly every pair of earrings in the store. Although she didn't buy anything, the attending clerk wasn't disappointed. That's because Jimmy Davis made a different kind of sale that afternoon. He secured Cleo Emily Lindsey's telephone number. Her number was something he coveted more than the commission he would make by selling her a pair of earrings.

He made a commitment to call her, and like every promise my father ever made, this one he intended to keep. As she walked out of the store, his eyes followed her.

He was so distracted that he forgot all about what he had been doing.

Jimmy had been with numerous women in Europe during the war, including some real beauties in England and Ireland. Now that he was living in a rural town like Cedartown, Georgia, he never considered it possible that he would meet the prettiest woman he had ever seen, but this was precisely what happened. Shaking his head in dismay, laughing at the irony, with no one to hear but himself, he muttered, "What are the odds?"

For a guy who had never had anything go his way, where not one thing in life had come easily, it was difficult for my father to accept that this was really happening.

As surprising as all of this was, he was even more astounded that a woman as beautiful as Cleo Lindsey was still available. Completing his winning trifecta, he felt certain she was as interested in him as he was in her. Sensing that the stars were finally aligning in his favor, he went back to work.

He called her later that evening, and the two made plans to have dinner Saturday evening, three days later. Apologizing that he didn't own an automobile, my father said that he couldn't pick her up. He asked if she would mind meeting him at the restaurant.

Fearful that she might reject him for this clear faux pas in etiquette, he was relieved when she consented without hesitation. Although Cleo still lived at home with her parents, she owned her own car. So, driving to the restaurant to meet him was perfectly amenable. After promising to meet at 7 p.m. that Saturday, they were equally as excited about their upcoming date.

Three nights later, Jimmy arrived at the restaurant at 6:45. He got there early just to make certain they would be seated without having to wait. Cleo arrived at 7:10, fashionably late. My dad wasn't surprised she would choose to be a little tardy. He expected it. Although not a college graduate, he had learned a thing or two about female dating behavior overseas.

When Cleo made her grand entrance, she was wearing a tasteful blue dress. It was sexy, but not too sexy. Seeing her, my father was dumbfounded. He couldn't believe how beautiful she was. He stood to greet her and, not knowing anything about her other than how gorgeous she was, he made a decision right then that this was the girl he was going to marry. Having made this determination, as premature as it was, every subsequent choice from that moment on was aimed at moving the ball forward and making his decision become a reality.

Guys are like that. They can be that impetuous, that foolhardy, never thinking a thing about it. Women, on the other hand, are almost always the polar opposite. I didn't learn this from my dad, though. I had to learn it on my own.

Although Cleo had no idea what had just transpired in her date's mind, she was busy appraising him as well. After taking a good, hard look at him, without providing the slightest clue that she was doing so, she made the determination that he was marriage material. Noticing everything differently from that point forward, scrutinizing every move he made, she was pleased by the way he behaved.

After sitting down, she initiated the conversation by asking what he had done in the war. During that era, this was the first question everybody asked. It was what people wanted to know, but my dad certainly didn't want to begin their relationship by telling her about the horrors he had witnessed in Europe. He felt certain that doing so, especially talking about his experiences at the death camps, would scare her off. Plus, it would have made their date depressing. He certainly didn't want that.

Instead, after telling her that he had entered the army as a private but ended up a second lieutenant via a field promotion, he carefully shifted the conversation to focus on her.

Since talking about herself was far more amenable to Cleo anyway, they spent the remainder of the evening talking about her life. By the time dinner was complete, Jimmy knew a great deal about the young woman he intended to marry.

She was the youngest of four siblings, the only girl. Her three brothers doted on her. They were almost as protective of her as her mom and dad.

Cleo had been born and raised in Cedartown. It was the only place she had ever lived. The town was a railroad hub, where boxcars were transferred from one train to another to arrive at their appointed destination. Her father was a conductor for the railroad and had been his entire career.

Her family was Roman Catholic, a rarity in the Bible Belt. There weren't many Catholics in North Georgia. The town only had one Catholic church. The small congregation was manned by one priest who served a handful of parishioners. My dad learned that Cleo's faith was very important to her.

Pointing to Jimmy's chest, she told him how much she liked his Saint Christopher medallion. When she said this, Jimmy instinctively touched it.

Then, refusing to dwell on the subject because she didn't want to seem too religious, she shifted the conversation. She told her date that she had just turned twenty-two.

Her age was perfect for Jimmy, who was now twenty-eight. Cleo, who was five foot five, had naturally blonde, shoulder-length hair. She had a spectacular figure, which she maintained by dancing frequently.

Hearing that she loved to dance as much as he did delighted my father. Although trivial by most standards, this was the one thing he wanted the most in a lifetime partner. She went on to mention that she had won several dance contests and an equal number of beauty pageants, most of them local but a few regional.

Jimmy loved everything she divulged. Genuinely interested, he pressed her for added details, which Cleo was delighted to provide. That he was such a good listener was surprising, but it piqued her interest.

She told him that she had even won some beauty contests before she was a teenager. This meant that, even as a child, she had always been pretty. A close family friend and neighbor, a man who was a professional photographer, had been taking photos of her since she was a preschooler. She had posed for him hundreds of times, which made her feel at home in front of the camera.

After graduating from high school, Cleo began working at the local furniture store, where she remained employed. Still living at home, the last of her siblings to do so, with her mother cooking her meals, washing her clothes, and cleaning her room, Cleo was quite content to stay where she was. She had no plans to move out, not until she got married.

Having mentioned the "M" word and being completely forthright, Cleo admitted that she'd dated quite a bit. Several men had been interested in her, but she made a point to tell Jimmy that none of her relationships had developed into anything serious. Although he wouldn't have been dissuaded even if she'd had a steady beau, by the expression on his face, it was obvious he was grateful to learn that she was completely available.

Noticing his relief, which any woman would as intuitive as most are, she could tell that he was just as interested in her as she was in him, perhaps more so. This was reassuring.

Upon finishing dinner and their conversation, Jimmy walked Cleo to her car. Opening the door, he gave her a fraternal hug and a kiss on the cheek. Closing the door behind her, their eyes locked just before she drove off.

As he watched her car disappear, a broad smile crossed his face. This was the girl for him. He was certain of it. She could dance, she was beautiful, and she was into him.

What more could he ask? She was everything that he wanted and needed, everything that he required.

Many men are this naïve, this simplistic about choosing a life partner. In a sophomoric, incredulous way, they convince themselves that everything will work out, that everything will be copacetic, regardless of what they do. My father was certainly one of these men.

Although I learned a number of valuable lessons from my father, how to choose a mate certainly wasn't one of them. I had to learn that one on my own, through trial and error, just like almost every other guy. That's the bad news. The good news is the choosing process can be a lot of fun.

While driving away, Cleo viewed Jimmy in her rearview mirror. Also smiling, she thought he had real potential, but there was one glaring red flag. He wasn't Catholic. Because he wasn't, she doubted their relationship would develop into anything meaningful. *What a shame*, she thought.

During this era, in the late 1940s and early 1950s, long before Vatican II, good Catholic girls never married non-Catholic men. Jimmy might have been certain about Cleo, but, although the chemistry between them was clearly off the charts, she was more than a little hesitant about him.

★ ★ ★

Not surprisingly, the attraction that existed between Cleo and Jimmy trumped her religious convictions, at least in the initial stages of their relationship. During the week after their first date, they spoke on the phone daily, sometimes for an hour or more at a time. Then, they dined together the following Saturday night. Eating more quickly on the second date, they went to a club to dance for the rest of the evening. That my dad's skill equalled hers at the jitterbug definitely pleased Cleo.

At the end of the evening, although both were sweaty from all the exercise, Jimmy kissed her. She liked that he did. Both wanted more but, out of respect, my dad refrained.

The following week, they replicated what they had done previously. This time at the end of the evening, while sitting in the front seat of her car, long before bucket seats became standard, Jimmy kissed her again, but this time he continued for quite a while longer.

When he did, the smoldering chemistry that existed between them burst into flames. Embracing each other closely for several minutes, things began to go too far, at least for Cleo. Unwilling to go all the way, she finally pushed her date away.

Looking at him with lipstick smeared all over her face and her dress discombobulated, she said, "I think it's time for you to meet my family."

Surprised to hear this, which was the last thing on my father's mind at the time, he responded, "Okay, that would be fine with me. When?"

"How about having dinner at my house Sunday afternoon—not tomorrow but the week after? Would you like that?" she asked.

"Of course I would," my father assured her. "I'd be happy to come."

"Great, I'll pick you up right after Mass. Can you be ready by one o'clock?"

"Absolutely, I'm looking forward to it."

The following Sunday, Cleo pulled up to Aunt Mary Jo's house precisely at 1 p.m. No longer feeling the need to arrive fashionably late, and punctual by nature, she was right on time.

My dad, who was rarely nervous about anything, had been anxiously pacing on the porch, smoking one cigarette after another. Seeing her drive up, he put out his smoke and walked to her car.

With a grin a mile wide, like he didn't have a care in the world, he said, "I'm ready."

As he eased into the car, it was obvious that she looked concerned about Jimmy meeting her family, especially her dad. She was also anxious about him meeting her three brothers, as protective as they had always been of her.

My dad was equally as nervous, but he needn't have been. His lengthy army tenure had made him a pro at getting along with guys his own age—and with older men too.

Engaging effortlessly from the moment he walked in the front door, my dad won over the Lindsey family quickly and effortlessly, especially Cleo's father. A gruff, burly older man, Homer Lindsey took to Jimmy immediately. Because her dad began teasing Jimmy right away, making both of them laugh, Cleo knew that her father really liked her newest boyfriend.

Endearing himself to all of Cleo's family, including her mom, by the time the pot roast was served an hour later, Jimmy had ingratiated himself to the entire family.

They said grace before eating. Although my dad had never done this before, he wasn't the least bit uncomfortable. Instead, he enjoyed it. It made him feel like he was with a real family, a genuine one. It was the kind of family he had always wanted to be a part of but had never been.

After dinner, Cleo's mother, Daphne, sat beside Jimmy on the sofa and smiled warmly. He could see that she was holding an album in her hand. She asked, "Would you like to see some photos of Cleo when she was growing up?"

"Yes, I would love that," my dad responded enthusiastically.

Turning to her daughter, Daphne suggested in an endearing tone, "Come sit next to me, dear."

"No," Cleo snapped frostily. "I don't want to see those pictures." Obviously miffed, she skulked out of the room a moment later, headed toward her bedroom.

Daphne didn't challenge Cleo's rude response. Neither did her father or her brothers. This surprised Jimmy a little. Apparently, Cleo's behavior wasn't unusual. To him, Cleo's reaction seemed excessive, but he chalked it up to her being modest about the photos.

Returning her attention to my dad, Daphne showed him page after page of photos, beginning when Cleo was less than five years old. Each shot was stunning, including the composition—professional in every way. My father thought the shots must have cost Homer a pretty penny.

In the early evening, when Cleo drove him back to Mary Jo's, my father leaned over and said, "I love you." It was the first time he had ever said this—at least, the first time he had meant it when he said it.

"I know you do, Jimmy. I love you too. I really do, but being in love isn't enough," she countered.

"Of course it is," Jimmy protested.

"No, it isn't," Cleo rebuffed.

"What do you mean?" he asked, clearly confused.

"It means that our relationship isn't going anywhere."

"I don't understand," Jimmy countered. "Why isn't it?"

Looking at him with tears welling up in her eyes, she confessed, "It's because I'm not going to marry anyone who isn't Catholic, that's why."

When she said this, Jimmy understood why she had remained available for so long. With so few Catholics in Cedartown, any relationship she might have desired was doomed before it even began, exactly like theirs appeared to be.

Nodding his head that he understood, my father looked into her eyes and asked, "Can we talk about this later?"

She agreed and kissed him on the cheek. Knowing not to be physical in any way, Jimmy simply slid out of the car and walked into Mary Jo's house. This time, he didn't watch Cleo drive away, which he had done religiously up to that point. She noticed, and it stung.

Although Jimmy wasn't about to give up on their relationship, Cleo didn't realize this. Based on her past relationships, she erroneously assumed that her beau had lost interest, but he hadn't. Nevertheless, what she said had given him pause. He needed time to think, time to reflect.

★ ★ ★

Their relationship had progressed fast, superfast, but this wasn't unusual, not during the era following the war. People didn't date nearly as much back then as they do now. Dating wasn't recreational. It was purposeful, aimed at leading to marriage, but that's not all. Once you were married, once you'd made a firm vow, a lifelong commitment, you honored it. There was no "maybe" in "till death do us part." My dad understood this and accepted it; so did Cleo.

From the time she walked into the Jewel Box looking for a pair of earrings, the two had spoken every day. To miss one day wasn't even a consideration. Speaking in the evening had become an integral, cherished part of their connection. Cleo counted on hearing from Jimmy and looked forward to his calls.

When she didn't hear from him that Monday, the day after meeting her family, she was crushed. Thinking the worst, she felt certain she had lost him. He didn't call on Tuesday either. By Wednesday, Cleo's mood had changed dramatically. With her dad gone, on a train headed to St. Louis and back, and her brothers living miles away from home, Cleo was stuck in the house with her mom.

Arriving home after work on Thursday to her mom serving leftover pot roast for the third night in a row, Cleo exploded. She threw her plate on the floor, breaking the dish and creating a huge mess. She was about to scold her mother mercilessly for not serving something different, but her harangue was interrupted by the telephone ringing.

Practically racing to pick it up, her rage ended as quickly as it began. Returning immediately to Southern gentility, she answered in her sweetest voice, hoping it was Jimmy.

"Hello," she said.

"Hi," my father responded warmly.

"Hi, yourself," she replied, grateful and relieved to hear from him.

Taking a deep breath, Jimmy said, "I've been thinking a lot about what you said. I know we need to talk, but not on the phone. Can we meet?"

"Yes," she replied enthusiastically.

"When are you available?" Jimmy asked.

"How about right now?" Cleo suggested.

My dad laughed. This made Cleo laugh as well.

"Okay, that will work," he replied. "Can you come on over?"

"I'll be there in twenty minutes," she promised. "I just need to brush my hair and my teeth."

Saying that she needed to brush her teeth was code. It meant that Jimmy needed to brush his teeth as well. She didn't like the taste of tobacco when he kissed her.

After hanging up the phone, she returned to the kitchen. Seeing her mother on hands and knees cleaning up Cleo's mess, feeling guilty Cleo said, "Let me help you with that."

"No, dear," Daphne responded kindly. "You go ahead. You don't want to be late."

Cleo brushed her teeth hurriedly, combed her hair, and put on lipstick and perfume. Then, she bolted out the door as fast as she could to see her beau.

True to her word, Cleo arrived at Mary Jo's house twenty minutes later. When she pulled into the driveway, Jimmy was standing on the front porch, but he didn't have a cigarette in his hand.

He walked directly to the car and got in. Sitting next to her, he reached over to hold her hand, but he didn't kiss her, which she expected. Instead, squeezing her hand gently, after taking a long, deep breath, he asked, "What do I have to do to become a Catholic?"

Catholicism actually resembles a
family that survives because,
even as it aspires to holiness,
it understands and can live with sin and imperfection.

EUGENE KENNEDY

Chapter 8

★ ★ ★

HIS FIRST HOLY COMMUNION

Who made us?
God made us.
Why did He make us?
To know, love and serve Him.
—ROMAN CATHOLIC CATECHISM

Three days later, Cleo drove to Mary Jo's house to pick up Jimmy. Once again, he had been invited to Sunday dinner with the Lindsey family. This time, however, Cleo didn't arrive at 1 p.m. Instead, she pulled up at 10:45 a.m. That's because Jimmy had promised to attend Mass with her. Having made the commitment to become a Catholic, it only seemed natural for him to accompany the woman he loved to church.

He wasn't the least bit hesitant about going. My dad was like that. Once he made a decision, he acted on it. He didn't wait, hem and haw, or vacillate—not about anything. After having made a decision, he did what he committed to do, never wavering.

This was one of his strongest character qualities. You always knew where you stood with Jimmy Davis. You never had to wonder. Being straightforward and purposeful were two of the things that made him so special.

Wanting to be exactly like my father, my hero, I began emulating his straightforward and purposeful traits at a very young age. I did this until these estimable qualities became as much a part of me as they were a part of him. Over time, they became solidly entrenched in me. Now, they have become hardwired. Like my father, not only do I never equivocate, I never mislead people. Everybody knows where they stand with me. They never have to wonder. Being forthright, precisely like my father was, has served me well throughout my career. It has been instrumental to my success.

That Sunday morning, when Cleo arrived, Jimmy greeted her with a passionless kiss—the kind married people give one other routinely. Then he got into the passenger side of the car.

"Are you ready for this?" she asked playfully, smiling at him. Her question was almost rhetorical, but not quite.

"Hell, yes," he affirmed. Pointing to the road ahead, he directed, "Forward, Jenkins," like she was his chauffer, which in many ways she was.

When the couple walked into the tiny church, arriving about three minutes late, Mass had already begun. This meant Jimmy didn't have time to say hello to Homer or Daphne. Cleo's three brothers, who lived in the nearby towns of Rome, Rockmart, and Coosa, attended Mass at other churches, but all three young men intended to be at their parents' house that afternoon for dinner.

Their mother told them dinner would be served at 2 p.m. Being of Dutch-German ancestry, when Daphne stated that their food would be on the table at a certain time, she meant exactly what she said. Always punctual, she was never late, and neither were her children. As a parent, she had successfully inculcated her promptness gene into all four of her offspring.

During Mass, when it came time to take Communion, Jimmy stood to go forward with the rest of the Lindsey family, but Homer told him to remain in his seat. He was not yet a Catholic, and Communion was closed to non-Catholics. So, it wouldn't have been appropriate for him to participate.

Once Mass was over, after taking a short walk, Cleo and Jimmy drove to her parents' house. As promised, dinner was served at 2 p.m. on the dot. This time, Daphne had smoked five racks of ribs, which she had purchased from a local farmer. She hoped she'd bought enough to feed five men and two women; she had, but it was close. There were no leftovers.

After dinner, while all five of the men were sitting at the dining room table, talking and smoking, Homer asked Jimmy what he thought about Mass.

Crinkling his brow, Jimmy said, "I liked the sermon, especially that it was short, but I couldn't understand what the priest was saying the rest of the time. It just didn't make sense."

When Cleo's dad and brothers heard this, they made eye contact with each other. Then, all four burst into laughter. It was so uproarious that Daphne and Cleo came into the dining room from the kitchen just to see what was so funny.

When the laughter subsided, Homer explained, "It's because the Mass is in Latin."

"Latin!" my father exclaimed, genuinely puzzled. "Why would it be in Latin?

"I don't know," Homer admitted. "Because it's always been in Latin, I suppose?"

This surprised Jimmy but, having already made his commitment, he didn't want to begin his conversion process by challenging Catholicism's tenets.

From antiquity, the Mass had always been said in Latin and would remain so until Vatican II. Throughout the ages, precisely like Jimmy's experience, Catholics had no idea what was being spoken.

At one point in the Mass, the priest turns around from the altar. When he does, he holds the Host up high. Then, he says loudly, "*Hoc est enim corpus meum.*" The Latin phrase means, "This is my body." Because it's spoken more loudly than the rest of the Mass, the parishioners twisted its meaning a little, coming up with, "Hocus Pocus." This idiom came to be a phrase commonly referring to something that is unintelligible, something that nobody could understand. For centuries, magicians have used this phrase in their magic shows.

Later that afternoon, after helping Daphne clean up after dinner, Cleo drove Jimmy back to the church. Waiting for him outside, Jimmy went into the church alone.

Having told the priest, Father Ronan Cunny, that Jimmy planned to convert, a meeting was scheduled. When my dad walked in, Father Cunny greeted him warmly. Then he handed him a copy of the Catholic Catechism.

"Just about everything you'll need to know is in this book," the priest said, smiling. "Study it. Learn it by heart if you can."

"I'll do my best," Jimmy responded.

"I'll guide you along the way and answer any questions you might have," Father Cunny promised. "If it's all right with you," he continued, "we'll have our first lesson now."

"That's fine," Jimmy responded. "Let's do it."

After the two sat down, Father Cunny opened to the first page and read, "Who made us?"

Seeing the answer beneath, Jimmy responded, "God made us."

"That's right, Jimmy. God made us. Do you believe that?"

"Yes, Father, I do," Jimmy acknowledged.

"Good, that's the most important thing you need to know. Don't ever forget that," the priest admonished.

Jimmy nodded in assent.

Next, Father Cunny asked, "*Why* did He make us, Jimmy?"

Again looking at the page, my father responded, "To know, love, and serve Him."

"That's right, Jimmy. Do you believe that as well?"

Jimmy paused for a long, contemplative moment. Then he replied, "Yes, Father, I do."

When my dad said this, he meant it. He internalized this truth at the core of his being. Our purpose in life was to know, love, and serve God. It was a lesson he never forgot; neither would I.

* * *

A month and a half later, on a warm Saturday afternoon, since Jimmy still didn't own an automobile, Cleo drove him back to the local parish. He had successfully completed his pre-conversion training. This meant it was time to make his first Confession. Realizing all that this would entail, he practiced what he intended to say.

Upon entering the Confessional, Jimmy did as he had been trained to do when the priest pulled back the sliding door that separated priest from penitent. Jimmy said, "Bless me, Father, for I have sinned."

Separated by nothing but a thin, dark screen, the priest replied, "What are your sins, my son?"

Without any prodding, my dad unburdened himself or, more accurately, unloaded on the priest. Holding back nothing, Jimmy let it all out. As a World War II vet, having tasted battle and the stench of death routinely, coupled with at least as many episodes of bacchanalia while on leave, I'm certain the hair on the priest's ears must have been singed by the time my father finished. Despite all the darkness, depravity, and evil my father had witnessed, despite all that he had endured and participated in as a GI, Father Cunny gave him absolution.

Once he did, this meant that former Second Lieutenant James Thomas Davis was eligible to make his first Holy Communion. Normally, even though children don't realize how significant this event is, most make their first Holy Communion when they are seven. My dad had just turned twenty-nine.

Although young kids aren't excited about anything involving church, their parents certainly are. Jimmy's parents weren't there to celebrate this event, though. With his mom having died more than two decades earlier from brain cancer and his dad probably sleeping off a night of drinking in the gutter somewhere, my father claimed Cleo and her family as his new kinfolk. That they were present meant the world to him. The proudest of them all was Cleo.

When my dad went forward, she was sitting in the first row to witness the event. To say she was proud of Jimmy would have been a massive understatement, especially knowing that he had done this for her.

Because conversion had been a requirement for Cleo to marry Jimmy, he had gone through a rigorous process to become a Roman Catholic. Now, nothing stood in the way of bringing their union to fruition. To not acknowledge that this was a motivating factor in his conversion would be misleading. Cleo understood this, but seeing Jimmy walk to the altar rail and kneel before God, precisely as he had been instructed to do, melted her heart, but it didn't melt her resolve.

As she watched him take the Host, she couldn't have loved him more, but love wasn't the only emotion she experienced that day. She also felt a deep sense of unworthiness. On the outside, as beautiful and sophisticated as she was, no one could have imagined how she felt on the inside, where it really counted. Cleo didn't consider herself to be a good person at all, quite the opposite. She didn't think she was good enough for Jimmy. Instead, she considered herself to be a shameful woman.

Jimmy didn't feel that way at all, especially after taking Communion. For him, what you saw was what you got. He was completely transparent. Despite being an orphan and a war veteran, none of his horrific experiences had broken him on the inside. He'd weathered each storm and every disappointment successfully.

Cleo admired Jimmy for being so resilient, but she knew she wasn't. Even if others couldn't see what she was really like, she knew. As transparent as Jimmy was, Cleo was equally as opaque. She kept secrets, deep, dark secrets, never confessing them to anybody—not to her family and certainly not to Father Cunny in the confessional.

She took Communion, but it never brought her peace. It never brought her comfort or contentment. Although she pushed the dark spots on her soul down as firmly as she could, repressing who she was didn't always work. The darkness inside of her frequently reared its ugly head.

Deeply disturbed, she felt that nothing, not even the depth of God's love, could cleanse the wounds that had engulfed her soul. Although she hid her wounded-ness masterfully, never allowing anyone to be privy to the secrets she kept, they were always there. Ever watchful, she refused to allow anyone inside. She wouldn't permit it. She couldn't.

Being beautiful and eagerly sought by men allowed her to display an elegant, enchanting veneer while simul-taneously permitting her to repress the rage that existed deep within. Her manufactured persona allowed her to be alluring and desirable while carefully camouflaging who she really was. She wanted to be what she portrayed her-self to be. She tried diligently, desperately to be that per-son, but she was never as successful as she wanted to be.

Her demons were too powerful. Their hold on her was too firm. Frequently rage-inducing, they required an outlet.

Even though she knew it was unfair to refuse to be completely forthcoming with Jimmy, Cleo just couldn't bring herself to be as honest as she needed to be. Because she couldn't, the love she felt for him that day, which was greater than anything she had ever experienced in her entire life, was offset by a hefty measure of guilt and self-loathing. She hated herself for not being as honest as she needed to be. Despite feeling this way, she remained silent.

This was the bad news. The good news was that Jim-my's love for her was what she had always desired. Long-ing for a worthy man to cherish her the way he did, she felt blessed beyond measure. He was committed to her and wanted to marry her. Despite everything, becoming his wife was also what she desired more than anything in the world.

* * *

Initially, my dad may have converted just to marry Cleo. Accepting that this was the case, before he received his first Holy Communion, his primary purpose expanded. His goal was no longer simply to marry the girl of his dreams. That's because, during his conversion process, my father became a Catholic, heart and soul. His belief system and worldview became aligned with his faith, producing a man who was a better version of himself than he'd ever thought possible.

It's not surprising that things happened this way. Thinking about it, such an outcome was predictable. Having been raised in an orphanage, where everything in his life was highly structured, my dad was used to conforming to a rigid set of rules. Deviation was never permitted.

His years in the army were even more highly structured. Military life was regimented, with no wiggle room whatsoever. A firm chain of command existed, where questioning authority was never permitted. My dad was required to conform, which he did dutifully. Doing so became second nature to him.

Catholicism was the same way. As highly defined and structured as it was, the faith appealed to a man like my father. Because he was used to obeying legitimate authority, he never considered Catholicism to be repressive—just the opposite, in fact. For him, it was freeing and liberating, particularly because his *Weltanschauung*—or worldview—became perfectly aligned with the Church's.

The Catechism taught that one's purpose in life was to know, love, and serve God. After witnessing the destructiveness of the war, coupled with the absence of any adequate parenting, to have his goals conform to God's will was very appealing to my father. This meant that being a Catholic came easily to him, even during a period when nativism in the South was commonplace.

As affable as he was, once people got to know him, they liked him, even if he was a Catholic.

Nevertheless, even with his newfound, unshakable commitment to Catholicism, Jimmy was still a man with normal desires. Cleo understood this. It would have been impossible to miss. Having accomplished what she'd required for their relationship to move to the next level, Jimmy wanted his reward. Who could blame him?

With racing hormones that required sating, coupled with the willingness to commit a mortal sin to go all the way with the woman he loved, Cleo knew she couldn't hold him off much longer. Besides, she didn't want to keep telling him no. Her desire equaled his, perhaps surpassing it occasionally, if that was possible. They were living in a powder keg, and she knew it.

For Jimmy and Cleo, heavy petting had become routine, but this wasn't enough. One evening, when it was everything she could do to maintain her boundary, not wanting to add another layer of darkness to her soul, she pushed him off.

Buttoning her blouse, she moved away. Then she said, "I want to ask you a question." Without waiting for him to respond, she continued, "What are you doing on September 20?"

After mulling it over in his mind for a moment, especially since the date was six weeks off, he replied, "I have no idea. Nothing, I suppose. Why do you ask?"

Emphatically, she stated, "Because that's the day we're getting married."

> *Desire is the key to motivation, but it's*
> *determination and commitment*
> *to an unrelenting pursuit of your goal,*
> *a commitment to excellence,*
> *that will enable you to attain the success you seek.*
>
> MARIO ANDRETTI

Chapter 9

★ ★ ★

HAVING FOUND
EACH OTHER

A successful marriage requires
falling in love many times,
always with the same person.
—Mignon McLaughlin

In all fairness to Cleo, her pronouncement that she and Jimmy were going to get married, flatly stated as a demand, was not a bona fide proposal. Despite this, my father would tease her about it, insisting that she had asked him to marry her, not the other way around. When he said this, it was always in a playful way. He was never serious. The truth is, from the time my father made the decision to become a Catholic, it was assumed by both that they would marry.

During this period, especially for veterans returning from the war, there was little interest among them in dating numerous women—not just dating for the sake of dating. Going out with women was not recreational, at least not for the majority. It was purposeful.

Having had their lives placed on hold, not knowing from one day to the next whether they would even survive, the brave young men who constituted the Greatest Generation weren't looking to elevate the number of women they bedded. Some did, but most had more noble aspirations. More than anything, they were interested in starting families, in creating stable homes, in producing offspring to carry on their names, and in leading normal, fulfilling lives.

Experiencing the horrors of global war for years, where want and scarcity dominated their daily routine, when they never knew where their next hot meal would come from, when they would have given a month's wages just to sleep in a warm bed for one night, their hearts desired normalcy. Lacking the opportunity to even defecate on a real toilet, they yearned for stability more than anything. They craved it. Having sacrificed a large percentage of their youth in the hope that their future would be better, they wanted to return to normal living as soon as the war ended.

Many already had sweethearts back home. Others, including my dad, had a vision for what they wanted their sweethearts to be.

At the macro level, American GIs fought so that their way of life would survive and they would never be enslaved by either the values of the Nazis or by Japanese imperialism. Our soldiers were overwhelmingly successful at achieving both of their goals. At the micro level, what nearly every soldier desired, what each fought to protect, was the ability to live in peace and to have a home, a wife, and children. Almost to a man—and for some women too—this was what their hearts desired more than anything else.

My father was no exception; neither was Cleo. Having found each other, formalizing their relationship by getting married was what both desired. When Cleo set an actual date, while they were amorously engaged in her car that evening, with the air as hot and sultry as their passion, Jimmy's intimate intentions subsided immediately.

Sitting up, moving all the way over to the passenger side, and resting his back against the door, Jimmy lit a cigarette. Then, smiling at Cleo after inhaling a long drag, he was aware that he had her full attention.

Crinkling her mouth just a little, she raised her eyebrow. "Well, what do you think?" she inquired, although she was absolutely certain what his response would be.

There was a lightness to the moment. Despite this, my father knew a serious response was required. Taking a deep breath, he said, "There isn't anything in the world I want more than to marry you. It's what I've always wanted."

A little surprised by the second part of what he said, she squinted her eyes, rhetorically asking him to elucidate.

Understanding her nonverbal question, Jimmy clarified. "In combat," he said, "when the outcome was uncertain, even though I didn't know much about God at the time, I asked Him, 'If You allow me to survive, I'll find the woman You have for me. I'll marry her, be faithful to her, and create a family that will be a much better one than the one I had.'"

Jimmy didn't tell her that his prayer also contained a repudiation of his father's example. Thinking it was unnecessary, perhaps even counterproductive, he omitted it. Becoming quite emotional, tearing up a little and finding it somewhat difficult to breathe, Jimmy paused for a long moment.

Wiping the tears from his eyes, he added, "When I found you, knowing who you were the second you walked into the shop, I knew that God had answered my prayer."

When Cleo heard this, she also found it difficult to breathe. She teared up. She was grateful that Jimmy loved her this deeply, but she felt unworthy of his adoration. Like a ton of bricks, a pang of despair overwhelmed her.

Unaware that she was conflicted, my father waited a moment for the woman he loved to regain her composure before he continued. "I love you, and I always will—no matter what," he said. "You can count on that. I promise."

Cleo didn't respond but, deep within her heart, she knew that he would keep his promise.

★ ★ ★

The following Monday, when Jimmy went to work at the Jewel Box, he had a smile on his face and an extra bounce in his step. Walking into the back room where his sister worked, he asked her if she would make a wedding ring for Cleo.

More than delighted to do this for the brother she loved so dearly, Mary Jo pulled together scraps from this and that, adding stones that looked more expensive than they really were. Putting other projects aside for the day, she created a ring in record time. When she was finished, she was pleased with herself. She had created a wedding ring for Cleo that was much nicer than anything Jimmy could have afforded, particularly if he had been forced to pay retail.

When Jimmy presented the ring to Cleo that Wednesday evening, doing so on bended knee in the traditional way, she was genuinely surprised—not that he would propose, but that he had such a nice ring for her. It was the one she would wear for the rest of her life. Once he placed it on her finger, she held it up, marveling at its beauty.

Despite Jimmy's assertion to the contrary, Cleo felt certain the ring was far more valuable than anything the young couple could afford. Nevertheless, she was delighted to wear it. My dad could see how much she admired it; it was obvious Cleo was as pleased as he hoped she would be.

Turning to him, she said, "If it's okay with you, I won't wear it until Sunday. After dinner, I'll put it on."

"Sure," my dad replied, but there was a hesitancy in his voice. It was obvious he didn't understand why she wanted to do that.

Explaining, Cleo said, "I want to surprise my family. Are you sure you are all right with me doing it that way?"

Loving the idea once he understood her reasoning, Jimmy smiled. "You bet I am. I can't wait to see the look on your dad's face."

★ ★ ★

After Mass, with Jimmy having taken communion with Cleo and her parents, the couple drove back to the family home. About an hour later, Cleo's three brothers arrived, just in time for dinner. It was served promptly at 2 p.m. As usual, the entire family was in attendance.

That afternoon, Daphne made fried chicken that was the best my father had ever eaten. To accompany it, she served rice and gravy, turnip greens with pepper sauce, a side salad, and peach cobbler.

By the time everybody finished stuffing themselves, all five men were ready for a nap, but dozing off wasn't in the cards, not that day. Excusing herself for a brief moment, Cleo went to her bedroom. When she left the table, she caught Jimmy's eye and winked.

Unable to maintain a straight face, being aware of what was about to happen, my father camouflaged his smile by wiping his mouth with a napkin.

Returning a short time later, without saying a word, Cleo held out her hand for all to see. Spotting the ring she was wearing, beginning with Daphne, who understood immediately what it meant, all of the Lindseys began to cheer.

As promised, my dad looked to see what Homer's reaction would be. Not surprisingly, Cleo's dad was as happy as he could be. Jimmy had hoped for this reaction, but he was grateful to witness the verification. Not having asked Homer for Cleo's hand in the traditional way, based more on circumstances than anything else, my dad was more desirous to have Homer's approval than anyone else's.

Everyone in Cleo's family loved my father. From the first time he'd come to dinner, they had been hopeful the two would marry. Now, their desire was about to come to fruition.

Jimmy loved Cleo's family as well, especially her dad. My father already felt like he was part of their family. That never changed.

After a brief time spent congratulating the couple, Cleo announced that the wedding would be held on September 20, just five weeks away.

Cleo's mother, a consummate organizer, turned her attention immediately to planning the wedding. Unlike Cleo, Daphne knew precisely what was necessary to pull off a successful wedding, with a reception to follow.

During this period, weddings were not the elaborate, ornate affairs they have come to be in the twenty-first century. Although lovely and joyous, they were much simpler. This didn't mean they were just thrown together, though. They simply didn't require a year—or more—of planning.

When Cleo told her mom that the wedding would be held five weeks later, Daphne thought that with a little bit of luck, she could pull it off spectacularly. Nevertheless, she didn't intend to allow any grass to grow under her feet. She needed to start planning right away.

Looking at her daughter, she said, "I'm assuming you want to get married on a Saturday afternoon. Is that correct?"

"Yes, Mom," Cleo affirmed.

"That would be Saturday, September 20?" Daphne asked.

Cleo nodded, affirming the date.

"Okay, that will work," Daphne continued, as the wheels in her head began to turn. A moment later, she said, "We'll need to make sure the church is available."

"I've already done that, Mom," Cleo stated. "And, before you ask, Father Cunny has already agreed to marry us." Cleo added this, knowing what the next question would be.

"Hmm, so Father Cunny knew about this before I did?" Daphne asked, a little perturbed by the slight, while simultaneously impressed that her daughter had the foresight to plan ahead, booking the church and the priest in advance.

"That's because I wanted to surprise the entire family at dinner," Cleo explained with just a hint of trepidation in her voice, knowing that her announcement had slighted her mother just a bit. "I wanted Jimmy to see y'all's faces," Cleo added. "I want him to feel completely welcome in our family."

"He is welcome, honey," Homer chimed in. "The way you did it was really sweet," he added, ending a potential mother-daughter conflict before it had time to fester.

Homer's affirmation of Cleo, which acted as a de facto rebuke to his wife but without the sting of an actual reprimand, changed the direction of the conversation, but the subject matter remained the same. There were numerous items that required addressing.

Speaking to herself more than anyone else, Cleo's mom said, "I'll need to think about what to serve at the reception." Looking at everyone at the table, she suggested, "I think we'll have a champagne toast to the couple. We'll also have one keg of beer. Nothing more, no hard liquor. I don't want anybody getting drunk and spoiling the wedding."

Looking from face to face, ending with her husband's, she asked, "What do y'all think? Is that all right with you?"

"Absolutely," Homer replied.

Everybody else agreed that this would be acceptable.

Pietism was not part of the Lindseys' faith, despite the fact that the wedding would be held in the Deep South, the buckle of the Bible Belt, where alcohol was routinely served at Catholic weddings. Even the priest would toast the couple with a glass of champagne. Father Cunny might also enjoy a couple of glasses of beer and have a cigarette with his parishioners. Such behavior was never considered unusual, and certainly not sinful.

Continuing with her planning, Daphne said, "I'll come up with the menu later. We'll need flowers." She added, "I think I'll go to Cartersville for them, maybe even take a trip to Lenox Mall in Atlanta."

Affirming his wife's plans, Homer said, "Whatever you think is best. You're the boss."

"Thank you, dear," Daphne responded. Looking at her daughter warmly, she stated the obvious in a loving way: "We only have one girl, you know."

Homer added, "And a very special one at that."

Smiling at her father, Cleo replied, "Thanks, Dad."

Snapping her fingers, Daphne remembered, "I almost forgot. We'll need a photographer. I'll call Lance Pervers in the morning. I need to make sure he's available."

"I don't want him, Mom," Cleo said.

"Why not?" Daphne asked. "Lance has been taking pictures of you since you were six years old."

"I know, Mom, but I don't want him," Cleo stated, this time more firmly.

"Well, I do," Daphne countered defiantly. "He's a close friend, practically part of the family. He's been around for nearly twenty years. He'd be insulted if we asked someone else."

"I don't give a shit what he would be, Mom. I'm not having him, and that's final," Cleo hissed. To emphasize her point, she swept her hand across the table, sending plates and leftover food across the room. Unapologetic, instead of staying to help clean up the mess she'd created, Cleo stormed out of the room. A moment later, in a fitful rage, she slammed the door to her bedroom, defying anyone to come after her.

A brief moment later, my dad rose to go after her, but everybody at the table warned him to leave her be.

"If you value your life," one of Cleo's brothers advised, "you'll wait until she calms down." Everyone at the table concurred.

Stunned, horrified actually, as my father witnessed the entire event, he wondered what had just happened and what had precipitated it. Reflecting later, he realized that he was the only one who was surprised by Cleo's outburst.

Although her parents and brothers didn't approve of what she had done, none of them were shocked by it either. Because they weren't, my father concluded that Cleo must have behaved like this before, perhaps often.

Cleo didn't come out of her bedroom for the rest of the day. She had picked up my dad at Mary Jo's, driving him to church and then to the Lindsey home. So, when it became obvious that she wasn't about to reappear, Cleo's father graciously offered to drive Jimmy back home.

On the way to Mary Jo's, Homer scrupulously avoided the subject of his daughter's behavior. It was almost like it never happened, which seemed bizarre to my father, and a little disturbing.

What my father witnessed that afternoon created quite an impression on him. As unexpected as his fiancée's temper tantrum had been, the fact that the rest of her family weren't nearly as disturbed by it as he had been was bothersome. My dad concluded that they had become used to such behavior. What other explanation could there be?

This episode didn't give my father pause, however, not for a guy who had survived fighting Nazi Germany for two years. The depth of his love for Cleo, along with the commitment he had already made to her, was much too powerful for him to back out or back off. Reconsidering wasn't an option. For better or worse, he was her guy, and that would never change.

Nevertheless, after witnessing her outburst, which didn't make a bit of sense to him, he was determined to understand the causal factor. There had to be something behind his fiancée's anger, and he was determined to discover what it was.

> *By all means, marry. If you get a good*
> *wife, you'll become happy;*
> *if you get a bad one, you'll become a philosopher.*
>
> SOCRATES

Chapter 10

★ ★ ★

I DON'T WANT
ANYBODY TO KNOW

You are only as sick as your secrets.
—ALCOHOLICS ANONYMOUS APHORISM

On September 20, 1948, on a hot, late summer afternoon at Saint Bernadette Catholic Church in Cedartown, Georgia, James Thomas Davis and Cleo Emily Lindsey became man and wife. The ceremony was officiated by Father Ronan Cunny. It was a semi-private wedding. The entire Lindsey family attended, as did their very close friends, but that was all. On Jimmy's side of the aisle, his sister, Mary Jo, was the only guest present. Neither of his brothers could make the trip from North Carolina, but both sent congratulatory telegrams. Not wanting to jinx his marriage, Jimmy didn't even bother to inform his father that he was getting married.

That day, Cleo was radiant. Wearing a long, strapless white wedding dress, which was a little before its time, the gown accentuated her beautiful bare shoulders. Finding the dress at a "nearly new" store, Cleo realized it had been created for a socialite. The frumpy debutante it had previously belonged to evidently didn't like the way it looked on her, but it looked fabulous on Cleo. So, she was able to get married in a designer gown that she could never have afforded otherwise.

Along with a veil and tiara to accentuate her gown, the ensemble made her beautiful, long, blonde hair look ravishing. All brides do their best to look perfect on their wedding day; Cleo succeeded. The overall effect of her ensemble was stunning.

Just twenty-two years old, she looked attractive enough to grace the cover of *Glamour* magazine. A few attendees actually gasped at her beauty when they saw her.

Jimmy's bride was well-tanned for the occasion. She made certain to be, going so far as to not spend much time with her fiancé in the days leading up to the wedding. Sitting out in her backyard for hours on weekends during August and September, rubbing baby oil tinged with iodine on her skin to enhance the sun's effectiveness, by the time her wedding day arrived, she was as bronzed as a Greek goddess. The contrast with her white gown was breathtaking to behold.

When Jimmy first saw her that day being walked down the aisle by her father, her appearance took the groom's breath away. He couldn't believe how fortunate he was. The former shoeshine boy and World War II combat veteran felt a deep sense of gratitude.

During Cleo's slow promenade down the aisle, instead of having her eyes focused forward like most brides, she graciously turned to look at nearly everyone in attendance. It was as if she were greeting each guest personally with a knowing, familiar smile. As she approached the altar, she turned her gaze toward her soon-to-be husband.

When their eyes met, it was obvious to Jimmy that Cleo's commitment to him would be unassailable. She would love him as much as he loved her. This meant their marriage would be solid, remaining firmly intact until death parted them. He felt certain of this.

Their commitment to each other was something both promised to keep, and they did. They became man and wife that day, and her new name would be Cleo Lindsey Davis from that day forward. Several years later, I would become her only son.

The reception that followed immediately after the nuptials was held in the church's recreation hall. Knowing that Daphne had prepared a smorgasbord of delectables for the occasion, with catering being the exclusive domain of the very rich in those days, everybody in attendance remained to eat.

Daphne, who had been busy in the kitchen for an entire week before the blessed event, cooked Southern. Fried chicken and ham were the two meats served. As part of the Southern tradition, she cooked enough to feed three times as many as attended.

Traveling to Atlanta a month earlier, she had placed an order for the flowers that filled the church and reception hall that day. She also ordered a bride's bouquet of white roses and gardenias, accented by baby's breath. The flowers were tied together with a beautiful white silk ribbon. When Cleo carried the bouquet, the subtle greenery accompanying the flowers made Cleo's wedding dress look even more elegant. The overall effect was spectacular.

Where the photographer was concerned, the bride got her way. Nobody in the family was willing to push back against her adamant refusal to engage Lance Pervers. Instead, a photographer from Cartersville was contracted. Although not as talented as Pervers, the man did a satisfactory job.

Pervers was a longtime friend of the family, so the decision to not engage him was difficult, especially for Daphne. Although she was used to seeing him routinely at the Winn-Dixie grocery store where they both shopped, she certainly didn't want to run into him. Pervers was single and, unlike Daphne's husband, did all of his own shopping and cooking.

The sting of this social faux pas was so significant that Daphne changed grocery stores. She began shopping at the Piggly Wiggly. At first, she didn't like having to do this, but after learning where everything was, she actually preferred the new store.

What she liked the most about Piggly Wiggly, other than their excellent produce, was that she never ran into Lance Pervers again. As time passed, with Daphne avoiding him scrupulously, their friendship soon became a thing of the past. Not long afterwards, Pervers moved away. Not having seen him for a while, the Lindseys were totally unaware that he had even moved. With him gone, the memory of their friendship soon became distant, eventually fading away completely.

* * *

After the wedding reception, Cleo and Jimmy got into her car and headed to Atlanta to enjoy a five-day honeymoon. Staying at the Georgian Terrace, having waited to be together for so long, they consummated their union immediately, doing so a second and third time just to make sure.

Waking up next to each other for the first time the following morning didn't seem nearly as awkward to Cleo as she had imagined it would be. In fact, having Jimmy beside her seemed completely normal and natural. Having mutually agreed that they would never kiss until after having had their coffee—and him also having a cigarette— brushing their teeth afterwards, this became their lifelong routine. They stuck to this decision, despite what couples do in the movies, believing that morning breath was not conducive to a healthy relationship.

Now together twenty-fours a day for the first time, they got along surprisingly well. Their only conflict concerned whether or not my father would wear a short-sleeved shirt. Cleo insisted that he wear long sleeves.

Although this might seem trivial, it wasn't. There was a reason why. Cleo hated tattoos, and my dad had one—part of one, anyway.

While on leave in France, between the battles he fought with the Nazis, my dad got drunk one evening. He was with a couple of his buddies, both of whom wanted to get tattoos, but my dad didn't. Despite being pressured to join them, he adamantly refused. Having had way too much to drink, which was standard for nearly all GIs on leave during the war, he passed out. Taking him to the tattoo parlor with them, his buddies had an artist create a dagger on my father's left arm.

When the tattoo artist was three-quarters of the way through, my dad woke up. Enraged by what had been done against his will, coupled with being the former welterweight boxing champ on his base, my dad pulled away from the artist and punched him in the jaw, knocking him out cold. Turning to both of his friends, he decked them as well, but the damage had been done. From that point forward, my father had an unfinished tattoo of a dagger on his left arm.

It looked ridiculous, especially to my mother. Not wanting to be embarrassed by it, she insisted that he wear long sleeves.

While my father's response at the tattoo parlor may have seemed a little over the top, it really wasn't, not during World War II. Violence was a part of life for those who fought in the war. They saw death, mayhem, and carnage routinely, sometimes daily. Fighting among themselves wasn't considered a big deal, either, whether taking or giving a punch. The following day, having sobered up, my dad's buddies weren't even mad at him. By the following weekend, all three, having forgotten their previous conflict, went out again to carouse and look for women.

The tattoo artist might have held a grudge. Who could blame him? Having recently been liberated from Nazi oppression by American troops, however, he wasn't about to complain about the behavior of a GI.

The tattoo artist was probably more understanding than Cleo. Dad having a tattoo, especially a fragmentary one, mortified my mother. To her, it seemed like something a redneck would have—not the man she had chosen to marry.

To hide the unsightly image, she insisted that her husband wear long-sleeved shirts, even when it was hot, like it was in late September. With air-conditioning not available back in those days, my dad wanted to wear short-sleeved shirts but, choosing self-interest over comfort, especially while on his honeymoon, he acquiesced. Years later, he had the tattoo removed, but doing so required seven painful surgeries.

With the first day of their honeymoon a Sunday, nearly everything was closed. Back in those days in the Deep South, businesses honored the Sabbath. With nothing else to do, Jimmy and Cleo went to the movies at the Fox Theatre, which was located directly across the street from their hotel. After seeing a double feature, *Black Narcissus* and *Body and Soul*, they got caught in a late-afternoon shower when they walked out of the theatre.

After getting soaked, they needed to change their clothes before going to dinner. Disrobing, one thing led to another. Several hours later, with the dining room having already closed, they ordered room service.

The following two days were a whirlwind. They had cocktails at Tongue & Groove, danced at the Red Peacock, and dined at Lulu's Bait Shack. They had a grand time, but what they did more than anything else, like all newlyweds, was spend time with each other. Despite my dad's willingness to risk engaging in a mortal sin to go all the way, thanks to my mom, they ended up doing things the right way. Not having a long engagement helped, but once they began the intimate part of their relationship, there was no question about their physical attraction being strong and fulfilling. It was. That never changed, not through the entirety of their marriage.

Checking out of the Georgian Terrace early Wednesday morning, they drove to Toccoa, Georgia, a small town just west of the South Carolina border and not far from Tennessee. After eating fried catfish, slaw, and hush puppies for lunch, they drove to Toccoa Falls, which was located just a few miles away. It certainly wasn't Niagara Falls, but when you are young and in love, which my parents definitely were, it didn't really matter where you were. Simply being together, knowing that their marital adventure was just starting, was more than enough for them.

Staying at a local motel that evening, at the end of their brief but wonderful honeymoon, Jimmy and Cleo returned to Cedartown to begin married life. They had rented a small house on the outskirts of town. Although the house was meagerly appointed, they were thrilled to be in their first home. The two could not have been happier.

They'd spent the entirety of every dollar they had accumulated, which wasn't much, on their honeymoon. Because they were broke, that Saturday they returned to work, Jimmy at the Jewel Box and Cleo at the furniture store.

* * *

Three weeks later, they were enjoying Sunday dinner with the entire Lindsey family. This became a tradition that would continue for years. After clearing the table and excusing herself, Cleo's mom retrieved an album of photographs from her bedroom, but these were new photos, ones nobody at the table had ever seen. They were the photos of Cleo and Jimmy's wedding.

Daphne had driven to Cartersville to retrieve them two days earlier. Her intention was to surprise Jimmy and Cleo.

The wedding album was a wonderful disruption to what normally followed dinner. Not surprisingly, the photos of Cleo were breathtaking. My dad didn't look that bad either. Looking through them for the first time was enjoyable, even for the guys.

After thumbing through quite a few photos, one of Cleo's older brothers said, "These pictures are great, Mom." Then he added, "I don't think Lance Pervers could have done a better job."

Hearing her brother say this, Cleo tensed, becoming as rigid as a mannequin, but just for a moment. Nobody but her husband noticed. The others were focused on the photos, scrutinizing the quality of each. Everybody at the table agreed that they were outstanding.

Continuing to guide the others through the album, Daphne turned the page, but my father's attention was fixated on his bride. Holding his breath, he wondered what would happen next. Would Cleo pitch another fit or not respond to her brother's comment?

A brief moment later, she smiled. Pointing at the following photo, she reengaged with her family, allowing her brother's comment to pass. None of those at the table noticed a thing.

Relieved that the potential for a second temper tantrum had passed, my dad pointed at the photo as well. Making a cute remark about it, everybody laughed, ending any potential awkwardness.

Later that afternoon the couple returned home, still full from Mrs. Lindsey's feast. After making love, which Jimmy and Cleo did routinely on Sunday afternoons, they took a long nap. Awakening before Cleo, my dad poured both of them a glass of sweet tea. Taking the beverages to the porch, he sat there and waited for his bride to awaken.

A few minutes later, she did. Joining him, she sat down to enjoy her tea. After taking a sip, she looked at her husband and said, "Thank you for not saying anything at my mom's."

Jimmy knew exactly what she meant—that he had been aware of her consternation when Lance Pervers' name was mentioned. She was grateful he'd allowed the potentially tense moment to pass.

My dad just nodded. Normally, he would have spoken, but he intuitively knew an important conversation was about to commence.

"There's something I need to tell you," Cleo admitted. Once she said this, tears welled up in her eyes.

Knowing not to prod but to instead wait patiently for her to divulge what she needed to say, my father remained silent. Suspecting what she was about to confess, he simply waited for her to regain her composure.

Still crying, Cleo was having a difficult time catching her breath. In a halting tone she finally said, "You know what it is, don't you?"

My dad just nodded his head that he did. As it turned out, he didn't.

A long moment later, after wiping her eyes several times, my mom took another sip of tea. Looking at her husband, she said, "When I was six years old, Lance Pervers molested me. He did this repeatedly, many times for many years."

Waiting for my dad's response—hoping he wouldn't go ballistic and fearing that he might reject her altogether—she sat still. She had a wounded, sad, imploring expression on her face.

Having suspected that she had been having an affair, and surprised that this wasn't the case, my dad didn't explode. That the woman he loved had been abused deeply offended him, though. Intuitively, he knew that remaining calm, continuing to maintain control, was the best way to react. Many men would have become unglued, but not my father.

Remaining calm in the midst of a storm was one of his greatest character qualities. He had been required to preserve his equilibrium as a small child at the orphanage, then forced to do the same thing when he found himself homeless at age seventeen. He'd also had to keep his cool as he dodged German bullets during World War II. Jimmy Davis had learned that, when adversity threatened to overwhelm him, he could never react emotionally. To have done so might have proven fatal. He was not yet thirty, but because of his life experiences he had developed the wisdom of a much older man.

Instead of exploding, instead of becoming indignant, instead of being filled with rage and plotting vengeance, when he heard about what Lance Pervers had done, Jimmy reached out to hold his wife. She was the important one, not the pedophile who had violated her. He was crystal clear about how valuable she was. She was the woman he had just committed to cherish for the rest of his life. So, he held her tightly in his strong arms. It was a gesture of complete acceptance. Demonstrating his love, he permitted her to cry nonstop for the next twenty minutes.

That he would allow her to do so provided Cleo with a cathartic release she had never before experienced. Obviously unplanned, his acceptance was probably the most loving response my father could have made. The net result was a deepening of their bond, of their love, and of the two becoming one flesh.

That Jimmy demonstrated such a powerful commitment to Cleo, loving her in all the broken places, may have been the greatest example of love and acceptance he ever modelled to my sisters and me. Honestly, we couldn't understand it at the time, but we definitely counted on it.

Especially in our younger years, it provided the stability we needed in our home.

Dad taught us that just because someone is broken, especially when the carnage is unjustifiable, you don't discard that person. Your love has to be deeper than your level of discomfort. To enjoy lasting relationships, this is what is required. Regrettably, it's a lesson that seems to have been lost in the twenty-first century.

Unfairly, Cleo's painful experiences produced overwhelming shame deep within her. Since the first grade, before any child should be exposed to the nature of evil, she had been forced to carry this guilt, this unfair burden. She bore it alone, but that's not all. Daily, as if she had been the one to have done the wrongdoing, she reproached herself. Her molestation made her feel like a worthless woman. She experienced bouts of depression instead of developing a positive self-image. Even as beautiful as she was, she considered herself to be ugly, someone unworthy of love or respect.

With such trauma from being violated repeatedly, she clung to her secret, refusing to reveal it, not to anyone, especially her parents. She never once revealed her violation during Confession either. She just couldn't.

Although she never wanted anyone to find out, she finally confided in her husband. Once she did, she regained her composure somewhat after crying on his shoulder for so long, and then she finally pulled away. Exhausted, she sat back, sighed, breathed heavily, and then finished her tea.

Looking at Jimmy, she admitted, "I should have told you before we got married. I know I should have, but I was afraid you wouldn't love me anymore."

Smiling, my father replied, "Honey, nothing is ever going to change my love for you—not this and not anything else."

"Do you promise?" she implored.

"I promise," my dad affirmed, nodding his head.

"I'm so ashamed, Jimmy," she admitted.

"You have nothing to be ashamed about," my dad asserted with conviction. "You were six years old."

"I know, but it was still my fault," she confessed.

"No, it wasn't," my dad replied firmly. Although he was surprised that she would feel this way, he shouldn't have been. Although irrational, this is the way most victims of sexual assault view their victimization.

"I've been so afraid, Jimmy. I couldn't tell anybody."

"I understand," my father replied as he continued to affirm her.

Looking at him sternly, becoming resolute, she said, "I don't want anybody else to know about this—not now, not ever!"

Hearing this, my dad sat silently, meditating about what she had just said. He remained quiet for what seemed like a long time. What he wanted to do was to confront Pervers. My dad wanted to beat him to within an inch of his life, but he also wanted his wife to continue trusting him, to have complete confidence in his acceptance of her. Maintaining her trust trumped everything else. Without it, they wouldn't have the kind of marriage either desired.

Finally coming to a decision, he looked at her and said, "Okay, you have my word. This will be our secret, just between the two of us."

Looking at him, she wanted to confirm what he had just said.

Realizing this, my dad smiled, crossed his heart, and replied, "Scout's honor."

> *Trust is the glue of life. It's the most essential*
> *ingredient in effective communication.*
> *It's the foundational principle that*
> *holds all relationships.*
>
> STEPHEN COVEY

Chapter 11

* * *

A FEW MOMENTS OF
DEPRAVED PLEASURE

The world is a dangerous place to live;
not because of the people who are evil,
but because of the people who don't do anything about it
—ALBERT EINSTEIN

My mom was born in 1927, two years before the catastrophic Great Depression began. Her molestation started in 1933. That was the same year Adolf Hitler came to power in Germany. Her defilement ended five years later, not because Cleo was finally able to stand up to her assailant but, more likely, because she became too old to interest him. Since Lance Pervers preferred younger girls, my mom simply outgrew his depraved penchant. Since pedophiles never change—being incapable of abandoning either their perverted cravings or the ability to be genuinely repentant—her violator simply moved on to his next, younger victim.

Consumed with shame and fear of rejection because of what had transpired for so long and internalizing the pain, my mother never came forward. She refused to ask for help. If she had, there's no doubt her father and brothers would have confronted the pedophile. In that case, there's no telling what would have happened. Rest assured, it wouldn't have been pleasant for Pervers.

This never happened, though. The police were never informed either. Nobody knew, except for the pedophile and his victim. My mother guarded their secret with her life.

The Lindsey family was oblivious about all of this, never thinking, not for a moment, that their precious daughter could have been sexually violated by a trusted friend of the family. Instead, the Lindseys continued to hold Lance Pervers in high esteem. It never entered their minds that he was as devious as the serpent in the Garden of Eden. They never considered him to be a carnal miscreant who would inflict a lifetime of pain on an innocent child just to achieve a few moments of depraved pleasure.

The psychological damage that resulted was profound. My mother desperately needed therapy, but during the Great Depression, when most Americans were barely able to put food on the table, counseling would never have been a consideration, not even if her parents had known what happened. During the 1930s, and for several decades that followed, almost nobody sought psychological help. If a person did and it became public knowledge, there would have been a significant stigma attached.

Seeing a shrink was a shameful thing to do, a behavior that was mocked and ridiculed. Therapy was something reserved for those who required institutionalization. It was never considered an option for normal people.

All of these things had worked against my mother being forthcoming. So, when she made the choice to reveal her deep, dark secret to my father, it was the riskiest thing she had ever done. As it turned out, it was also the wisest decision she ever made. Wanting to be open and honest and desiring to have a solid relationship with her husband compelled her to do so. Besides, trusting him was part of the marital commitment she had just made. She considered it to be keeping her vow to love and honor him.

My dad was equally committed, having made a similar promise to her. Like his lifelong commitment to Catholicism, he took his wedding vows seriously. He had promised to love her "in sickness and in health," and he intended to do just that.

Through no fault of her own, Cleo had been wronged. The victimization cost her dearly. Something inside of her broke, and it adversely affected her for the rest of her life. It was so significant that, despite my dad's best efforts to help, her trauma would never completely heal.

Divulging what happened was helpful, but it wasn't nearly enough. Being traumatized at such a young age produced significant dysfunction. In many ways, her personal development became stunted from the time her molestation began, when she was just six years old.

Although she continued to mature physically, emotionally she remained quite young. In today's terms, what she experienced would be called arrested development. In the late 1940s, when she opened up about her molestation to my dad, almost nobody knew what that was. Jimmy Davis certainly didn't. What he did know was he needed to be protective of his wife, and that's what he intended to do.

Cleo's arrested development created problems, significant ones. Lacking the tools to deal with many of life's situations normally, she couldn't handle everyday events in a mature, healthy way. When things didn't go her way, she lashed out, verbally wounding those around her. When this happened, it wasn't pretty. She could be quite harsh.

Although a beautiful, engaging woman in her twenties on the outside, on the inside, parts of her had the maturity of a six-year-old. Instead of developing the skills necessary to deal with conflict in a healthy, normal way, she punished those around her, scolding and attacking them verbally, often throwing tantrums. Those who loved her, except for my father, paid a heavy price for their loyalty.

As the only one who understood the background behind her behavior, my father was able to help. He was capable of comforting her and calming her down. He was the only one who could, probably because he was consistently gentle, loving, and affirming.

He was also strong. Where Cleo was concerned, he was like a stake in the ground—firm and immovable. She was like a tetherball, flying around in different directions, never the same from one moment to the next. He kept her as centered and as functionally stable as he could, but it wasn't an easy task.

My dad never violated my mom's confidence, so she continued to trust him completely. He was her pillar of strength, her knight in shining armor.

I came to know and understand what had happened to my mother in an entirely independent way years later. I didn't learn it from my father. To have betrayed her confidence, even to his only son, was something he would never have done. A man of profound integrity, such perfidy was not in his character.

My dad didn't teach me to be loyal. He never needed to. Because that's who he was; I learned from his example. At a very young age, I understood that this character quality was an essential ingredient to be the kind of person God created me to be. My dad molded loyalty into me through example, which I believe is clearly the best way to possess it.

I'm glad I eventually learned the truth about my mother. It provided me with a better understanding of who she was. It also permitted me to see her from a more compassionate perspective than I would have otherwise.

★ ★ ★

While Jimmy and Cleo were still young newlyweds, with no children to deal with, they didn't experience many problems. They used this time to solidify and build their relationship. With no television to distract them, since TV was expensive and in its infancy, they spent most evenings enjoying each other. These were their golden years.

When Jimmy Davis returned from active duty and began working at the Jewel Box in Cedartown, he was essentially the store's custodian, the person tasked with sweeping out the place. That was just one of his responsibilities. He was also the stock boy and the person who displayed the jewelry when the store opened up. Then, to guard against theft after the store closed, he was responsible for placing the valuable items in the safe. Because he was so pleasant and friendly, he ended up waiting on customers as well. Not surprisingly, he was an excellent salesman. The store's profits increased because of his effectiveness.

Originally a marginal employee, perhaps hired simply because he was a war veteran, he soon became indispensable. This was due to his extraordinarily strong work ethic. He never slacked off. If there was nothing to do, he would find something. While at work, the job always came first. There was never a day when he didn't earn his keep.

Learning the jewelry business from the ground up, doing whatever was required to make the store thrive, Jimmy Davis ensured that the Jewel Box continued to be profitable. Eventually, his loyalty to the company, coupled with his outstanding work ethic, earned him a promotion.

He was named manager of the Cartersville store in 1951. With a population of about 7,500 people, Cartersville was nearly twice the size of Cedartown, making it seem like Metropolis to my father. This meant there would be twice as many customers. As Cartersville was quite a bit closer to Atlanta, an occasional shopper from the big city would drop in.

Thirty miles away from the Lindseys' house in Cedartown, Cartersville was just far enough away for my parents to be completely on their own, while also near enough for them to attend family dinners most Sunday afternoons. In the South, especially in rural areas, having every member of the family attend Sunday dinner after church, usually at their parents' house, was customary.

Sunday mornings, Jimmy and Cleo attended Mass at St. Francis of Assisi Catholic Church. In Cartersville, even though there weren't many Catholics, there were enough for the parish to have two services. Cleo certainly didn't have to drag Jimmy to church with her. When he became a Catholic, he embraced the faith. His conversion wasn't marginal. It was as solid as a rock.

Attending the early service most Sundays afforded the couple ample opportunity to arrive at Cleo's parents' house in time for dinner. Since Daphne continued to serve her meals promptly at 2 p.m., my mom and dad knew better than to be late, especially when fried chicken was served. If they arrived late, all of their favorite pieces would have already been taken.

Now a married woman, my mom was expected to bring something to add to the meal, which she always did. She never resented doing this. Although customary, it was also a labor of love. While at the dinner table, the men cut up with each other all the time. Everybody loved Jimmy, especially Cleo's dad. The two got along famously. Having been deprived of a family his entire life, my father loved these gatherings more than anyone. For him, Sunday dinners were like manna from heaven.

All of the Lindseys were proud of my father's promotion. Being the manager of a larger, better-stocked store meant my dad made a good bit more money. Having additional income permitted the couple to purchase a small house. As it turned out, it was a very small house—a two bedroom, one-and-a-half bath dwelling on Jones Mill Road.

As homeowners for the first time, they were ecstatic, especially my dad. Now in his early thirties, having been raised in an orphanage, this was the first permanent dwelling place he had ever experienced. Along with his desire to be a father and a college graduate, owning his own home—a place where he couldn't be thrown out—had always been a driving force in his life. Now, his dream had come to fruition.

Soon after moving in, my mom and dad made the decision to start their family. Having practiced the rhythm method successfully for several years, which required abstinence during ovulation, my mom never became pregnant. This was the method they used, since birth control was strictly forbidden by the Church. Using a prophylactic was also considered a mortal sin. Although the rhythm method didn't work for every couple, it did for my parents.

Once they stopped worrying about Cleo's periods of ovulation, my mom became pregnant almost immediately. My parents had moved into their house at the first of the year, and my older sister, Claire, was born on November 11, 1951.

A year and a half later, on July 13, 1953, I came into the world. Two and a half years after me, my younger sister Marie was born.

Both my mom and dad wanted a large family, and they got one. All five of us lived in the two-bedroom house on Jones Mill Road. With three children, they could have used a much larger place, but this house was all they could afford.

As kids, we didn't know the difference. Being squeezed together in one bedroom didn't bother us. It seemed normal. Claire, the oldest, had her own bed. Marie and I shared a bunk bed. She slept on the top. I slept on the bottom.

Although cramped, my memories of life in that house—especially of the love my father had for all three of his children—became the cornerstone, the building block, of who I would become. Although there was no "white privilege" involved, none that I can remember anyway, I loved my childhood. The times were hard, but we were fiercely loyal to each other. We had a great family life.

We loved Cartersville too. There's nothing better than growing up in a small town. People living outside of cities complain about it all the time, but they always seem to look back on their experiences nostalgically. Towns like Cartersville produce the kind of families that are the strength and backbone of our great nation.

My third sister, Therese, was an afterthought. My parents returned to the rhythm method after three children. Perhaps Therese's conception was a missed calculation about when ovulation occurred. Despite being a surprise, when she arrived on June 13, 1960, she was definitely wanted and loved. By that time, however, many things had changed, and not all of them were good.

The family is the first essential cell of human society.
POPE JOHN XXIII

Chapter 12

★ ★ ★

HIS PURPOSE WAS TO HELP US LEARN

It is only through labor and painful effort,
by grim energy and resolute courage,
that we move on to better things.
—THEODORE ROOSEVELT

Life is full of challenges. Some, like being compelled to fight in World War II, presented dangers that were difficult but unavoidable. Others, like having a family of five living in a two-bedroom house, needing to bathe daily in the same tub, created a much different set of stresses. In our family, which included three small children, the daily pressures of child-rearing brought out who my parents were—the good, the bad, and the ugly.

Back when they were dating, while enjoying several years as a childless married couple, maintaining their equilibrium wasn't terribly difficult—at least not as difficult as meeting the constant, never-ending requirements of attending to small children. As all parents come to realize, when kids arrive, who they really are becomes evident. It's unavoidable.

This was certainly the case where Claire, Marie, and I were concerned. We loved both our mom and our dad wholeheartedly and were devoted to each, but there was definitely a difference in the way the two of them treated us.

Dad was strong, firm, and loving. He was always smiling and joking with us. Regardless of how busy he was, he always made time for us. We brought him joy. Unlike the way his father felt about him—that he was a nuisance—we were never considered an unwanted burden, not by Jimmy Davis.

As I reflect on the days of my youth, I've come to believe that I had one of the best dads of all time. I'm convinced of it. Plus, I feel certain that he behaved the way he did for one reason: He was determined to give us a better, happier, more fulfilling upbringing than the one he'd experienced.

At one time or another, nearly every child makes a commitment to "never be like" his or her mom or dad, only to learn later in life that their parenting style is far too similar to what they said they abhorred. My father, unlike many, broke the cycle of neglect and parental disregard. His determination to never be like his own father motivated every parenting decision he made. Along with my mom, we were number one in his life, his first priority, the center of his universe.

He never wanted our childhood to resemble his. His father had never wanted him, but our dad always wanted us. Jimmy's existence—Frank and Robert's too—was considered an unwanted annoyance to Edgar Davis. By way of contrast, our existence was something our dad cherished. We were his pride and joy. He loved us. We knew it down to the molecular level. The thought that he might not love us never crossed our minds.

This was the legacy he bestowed on us. Our inheritance was that we were valued, not material possessions. Our white privilege was to be blessed by him and to learn from his leadership. The value of what he did for each of his children cannot be measured financially.

To be the recipients of this guidance was the cornerstone of all our accomplishments. Without it, I'm not certain I would have ever succeeded at anything. That's how significant his leadership was. It's why I consider the message of this book to be so important. It's also why I'm passing what I've learned along to others.

Where our mom was concerned, our experience was entirely different. There was no doubt that she loved us, but none of her children were comfortable around her. While our father was stable and steady, our mother wasn't. There were times, quite a few of them, when her behavior became volatile and unpredictable.

We never knew where we stood with her. One minute she was fine, the next she wasn't. Her mood fluctuations were so extreme that we felt like we were constantly walking on eggshells. Fearful and wary of her explosiveness, we did everything we could to avoid igniting an episode. We considered pacifying her to be our responsibility.

Occasionally, for no discernable reason, she would fly off the handle. Screaming at us, she would throw dishes or whatever else she could get her hands on. Like playing a game of dodgeball, we learned to get out of the way of flying objects. Although she never did any of us physical harm, we were always fearful that she would.

You might expect someone like this to be slatternly, to be unkempt, but she wasn't. Daily, she dressed well. More accurately, she dressed to the nines. Wearing a fashionable dress and heels, accented by a pearl necklace and matching earrings, she resembled June Cleaver on *Leave It to Beaver*. Often, she behaved like Beaver's mom—kind and understanding. Other times, she behaved more like Cruella de Vil, the villainess in *One Hundred and One Dalmatians*. We never knew which one would be making us dinner. Constantly on our toes, we were uneasy, always wary of her in our own home.

Perhaps some of her rage came from her inability to deal with the loss of her parents. My grandfather, Homer, died of cancer when I was just five years old. His absence seemed to add to Mom's stress, especially because she was raising three active children. She missed her father terribly. My dad missed Homer too.

When my grandmother Daphne died of cancer two years after her husband, her passing was even more difficult for my mom. Losing one's mother is never easy. Daphne's death ended the tradition of afternoon gatherings for

Sunday dinner. This was difficult for all of us, especially for my mom.

With both of her parents gone, Cleo became even more dependent on my father for psychological support. This didn't seem to faze my dad, though. He continued to be my mom's stable, immovable rock, always available, always nurturing, and always compassionate.

Whenever we were with my father, we felt safe. Whenever we were with my mom, we didn't. Even as small children, we felt required to parent her, doing everything we could to prevent her from exploding. Her outbursts were unpredictable, often coming out of nowhere. To my sisters and me, they seemed random, never purposeful. Where she was concerned, there was no rhythm or reason to anything.

With my dad, everything was the exact opposite. Rarely petulant and never peevish, he was the Rock of Gibraltar. Everything he did had purpose. Although a firm disciplinarian, he never flew off the handle. His corrections and reprimands were designed to teach us lessons about life.

His insights became our chief learning tools while growing up. His corrections were focused. They guided us so that we would learn how to become capable, competent adults. He taught us to live life with purpose, integrity, and definable goals.

Even though my dad experienced almost no fathering of his own, it was obvious he knew what he was doing. Realizing that there was intention behind his discipline made it much easier to accept his correction.

Our mother's discipline was different. Completely random, chaotic, and nonsensical, it felt like the goal of her discipline was to hurt us, not to teach us. Because her reprimands were punitive, they made us resentful. Mom was much harder on my sisters than she was on me. I'm not sure why, but she was.

Dad was different. He was always in control. Far too often, our mother wasn't. When my dad taught us a lesson, his purpose was to instruct us in how to be better equipped to deal with life on life's terms.

Because I was my father's only son, he focused on me more than he did my sisters. His goal was to make me a better man, and it worked. His lessons have never left me. They've become indispensable, helping me to become the man I am today. His leadership style, which I can remember from the time I first began to reason, produced indelible values that have become my core convictions. Not only did these values make me be a better man, they also made me a far more successful one.

I was seven when I received my first lesson. I remember how old I was because the events surrounding it occurred shortly after I made my First Holy Communion, which I received as a seven-year-old.

A boy down the street, Ernie, picked on me regularly. He was a bully, and I was scared to death of him. One day in our front yard, he was meaner to me than usual. He taunted me and hit me repeatedly, doing his best to provoke me into a fight, but I was too scared to stand up for myself.

When my younger sister Marie saw what he was doing, it made her mad. She told him to stop picking on me, but that only made matters worse. Becoming furious with Ernie, even though she was just four years old, she tackled him, got on top of him, and started hitting him. Finally pushing her off, Ernie cried and ran home.

That evening when our dad came home from work, Marie ran out to greet him. She yelled proudly, "Daddy, Daddy, I saved Tommy today!"

Surprised, he asked her what had happened, so she told him. After changing his clothes and pouring himself a glass of sweet tea, my father called me into the kitchen. Sitting me down at the table, he asked me why I hadn't stood up for myself and why I'd allowed my little sister to do it for me.

I admitted that it was because I was afraid of Ernie, and my dad nodded his head. A moment later, he said, "Call Ernie right now and ask him to come over."

"Why?" I asked, fearful of how Ernie would respond but even more fearful of what my father would do to correct my cowardice.

Answering, my dad flatly stated, "Because you're going to punch him in the face, that's why."

I was petrified—scared shitless, actually. Although trembling on the inside, I did exactly what my father told me to do.

A few minutes later Ernie came over. Standing in front of him in my driveway, I punched him in the face, just like my father told me to do. When I did, Ernie didn't hit me back. Instead, surprised, stunned, and hurt, he ran home crying. He never bullied me again.

What I learned that day was that even if someone is bigger than you, stronger than you, and meaner than you, you can never allow that person to intimidate you. You can never permit a person like this to bully you, to make you subservient to their mean-spirited demands.

I learned this lesson early in life, but it has always stuck with me. Now a senior citizen, I've never forgotten it. From that day forward, standing up to bullies and never allowing them to intimidate me, especially in my business dealings, became indelibly etched in my brain.

Incidentally, when we became teenagers, Ernie and I developed a solid friendship.

A year later, our family finally moved to a bigger house. It was on Grandview Drive. My dad, some of his friends, and I built a room for me in the basement. I loved it down there, especially when my mom would throw one of her tantrums. Retreating to my room, where she never came, I was safe and out of range. My sisters, whose rooms were on the second floor, weren't nearly as fortunate. They felt the full brunt of her fury and vicious verbal assaults.

Even when my sisters and I were teenagers, we had no idea what was behind her unstable behavior. Once a tantrum commenced, however, we knew it wouldn't stop until our father came home. As part of her acting-out behavior, profanity and throwing dishes were her weapons of choice. She could string a sentence of expletives together that would be the envy of any sailor. A master at using the f-word, her vulgarity was scary, but her ability to cuss was also impressive.

When my dad finally arrived home, he would assess the situation and then gently lead his wife into their bedroom. After shutting the door, he would quietly soothe her until she regained her equilibrium. He was the only one who could calm her down. As it turned out, his efforts were just a Band-Aid, never getting to the root of her problem. Nevertheless, from our perspective, his presence was a lifesaver.

★ ★ ★

Because I was my father's only son, he spent more time with me than with any of my three sisters. He did this not because he loved me more, but because he believed that my greatest responsibility in life would be that of a provider. In the third decade of the twenty-first century, this belief might be considered sexist, but not to those in the Greatest Generation. For them, being the breadwinner was always the responsibility of the man in the family.

Because of this, he wanted to make certain I was prepared to do my duty when I reached manhood. So, to begin my apprenticeship as a breadwinner, he wanted me to start making money at an early age. When I say early, that's exactly what I mean. With my dad's encouragement—which felt more like a demand—I was just eight years old when I started my first business.

I had no idea where to begin, nor did I receive any direction from him. I was on my own. It was my responsibility to figure out what to do, so that's exactly what I did.

I went into the landscaping business, which in those days meant I mowed people's lawns. Going door-to-door in the neighborhood, I got nine of our neighbors to be my customers. I promised to mow their grass for three dollars each, which meant I would make twenty-seven dollars a week during my summer vacation. That was big money in the early 1960s.

When I told my dad what I had done and how much I would make, I thought he would be proud of me. He was, but he also injected a little financial reality into my business plan. Since my enterprise depended on using the family lawnmower, he informed me that I would need to rent it from him. The charge for renting it would be one dollar per yard.

I hadn't figured on that, but I agreed. This meant I would only make two dollars a yard, but that was still a lot of money. Then, he said I would also need to buy my own gasoline. I couldn't use the gasoline that was in the can in the garage. That was his gasoline, not mine. I hadn't figured on that, either, but I offered to pay him fifty cents a yard for the cost of gasoline, which he accepted.

This cut deeply into my profit margin. Since Dad would get half of the money I made, it felt like I was in partnership with him. I didn't really like that, especially since I was the one doing all of the work, but I had no choice in the matter. In my eight-year-old mind, it seemed like I was getting screwed by my own father. I felt this way for a long time, but that wasn't the case.

Obviously, my dad didn't need my money, but he knew I needed to learn a valuable lesson. There was a cost involved in doing business. This lesson, as simple as it may seem, is one that many never learn adequately. I certainly did, and I was only eight when I learned it. I never forgot it either.

At the time, I resented only making $13.50 a week instead of $27, but that was still a lot of money. The lesson I learned from having to share what I earned, to quote an old commercial, was "priceless."

Having worked for a large corporation, as well as having been in business for myself for many years, the lessons I learned have always stuck with me. Without having learned them adequately, I wouldn't have been nearly as successful as I have been.

My father also taught me to work hard and to never disparage anyone who made an honest living, especially those who work with their hands. A good dad will tell his son or daughter to always honor those who work hard. A great dad will reinforce this by making certain that his children have "hands on" experience performing manual labor.

My dad was one of the great ones. One year, my summer job was to pick cotton. I'm not kidding. I spent my entire summer vacation in the hot Georgia sun picking cotton. It was the hardest, most difficult job I have ever done. The worst part, other than only receiving ten cents for every pound of cotton I picked, was that I couldn't wear gloves while I was working. Picking cotton barehanded, my hands were constantly receiving cuts. They were bloody from the day I started until two weeks after I returned to school. Those painful lesions required that long to heal. Most kids hate for their summer vacations to end—not me. That year, I couldn't wait to go back to school.

My dad wanted me to learn the value of doing menial labor, like what he was required to do shining shoes. He didn't insist I pick cotton as a punishment. It was to teach me to respect and value those who work tirelessly for minimum wage.

Obviously, this was a painful lesson to learn. Tough love always is. Ever since that job, I have never looked down on anybody who does menial work to make an honest living, not once. Unlike my father, who saw no end in sight when he began shining shoes, at least I was able to count the days until my summer job ended.

The following summer, my dad secured a job for me as a ditchdigger. Again, this was grueling work, but it also helped me develop core strength that has served me well ever since. Back then, parents used to frighten their children by saying, "If you don't go to college, you'll end up being a ditchdigger." Having worked an entire summer digging ditches, I can personally attest to the verity of this admonition. I definitely didn't want to make a career out of it.

There were other lessons I was required to learn as well. From the time I was very young, probably before I even started school, I was taught to never hit a girl. This message was inculcated into my brain repeatedly and adamantly. I knew and understood it well.

Despite this, one day when I was about fifteen, my younger sister Marie had been bugging me all afternoon. She was really getting on my nerves. When she saw how much she was irritating me, instead of stopping, she doubled down on her efforts. Sisters can be like that.

Finally, in an attempt to get her to stop, I punched her on the shoulder—not solidly, but not lightly either.

Stunned, she stood still in disbelief for a brief moment. Then, letting out a blood-piercing, hysterical shriek, she raced into the house to find my father. Before she was out of sight, I wished I hadn't done it, but there was no turning back.

A short time later, my father came into my room. I could tell by the look on his face that he meant business. He was pissed. Walking up to me, he asked, "Did you hit your sister?"

"Yes, Daddy, but . . ."

The next thing I knew, he hit me on the shoulder, right where I hit Marie, but his punch was a boxer's. It was much harder than what I had done, and it hurt like hell.

"How do you like that?" he asked.

"I don't," I admitted, rubbing my shoulder profusely.

"Then don't ever hit your sister again," he demanded.

"I won't," I promised, and I never did. In fact, the thought of ever hitting a female again never entered my mind. I had definitely learned my lesson.

My dad hit my shoulder hard, but it wasn't with all his might. I know this because I saw him hit a guy with full force once. It happened at an Atlanta Falcons football game.

My dad loved pro football, especially our home team. The guy sitting behind us was loud, drunk, and extremely obnoxious. Much younger than my father, the man began to taunt my dad, and he wouldn't let up. My dad tried to ignore him, but that didn't work.

Finally challenging my father, the two stood up. I'm sure the guy thought he would clean the floor with my dad, who had to be twenty years older, but that didn't happen. Instead, my father—the former welterweight boxing champion at his army base years earlier—hit the guy once in the mouth. When he did, the young man's knees buckled and he fell to the floor, out cold.

When the stadium security team arrived, they began to take my father away, but the people around us came to his defense. The fans told the security team that it was the other guy's fault, and the guards eventually took the bully away instead.

To everyone around us, my father was a hero, so we were allowed to remain and watch the Falcons get defeated. They've been doing that regularly for decades, even back then.

Perhaps my greatest lesson occurred when I was sixteen. Thinking I was all that and a bag of chips, I got drunk one Saturday evening. While driving home, I was pulled over and given a field sobriety test, which I failed. I was arrested and taken to the Cartersville police station.

Since everybody in town knew who my father was, instead of locking me up after booking me, which I deserved, they called him. When he came to pick me up, he definitely wasn't pleased.

Although he did the work behind the scenes to make certain the arrest wouldn't follow me the rest of my life, he made me do everything else that was required to handle my problem, including paying the bill for my lawyer. In all, I had to pay over five hundred dollars, which was a huge chunk of money back then. It took me forever to work off my debt. After that, I never got behind the wheel again after having more than two drinks. My lesson was expensive, but it worked, precisely as my father intended it to.

During my youth, I really didn't understand the importance of what I was being taught. Kids almost never do. Understanding requires time. My wisdom came later, sometimes years later, but the value from the lessons always materialized. My hope was that my father would be able to continue teaching me about life for decades more, but this was not to be.

Tell me and I forget.
Teach me and I remember.
Involve me and I learn.

BENJAMIN FRANKLIN

Chapter 13

IT WASN'T LIFE-THREATENING

When wealth is lost, nothing is lost;
when health is lost, something is lost;
when character is lost, all is lost.

—BILLY GRAHAM

As the manager of the Jewel Box, Jimmy Davis made the store very successful. Years earlier, after returning from the war, he began making a living by sweeping the floors and stocking the shelves in the Cedartown store. Having no career plans other than to find a wife and have a family, once he became involved in the jewelry business, he dug his feet in and never changed course. As a result, he became a first-rate gemologist.

Once he became the manager of the store in Cartersville, he almost immediately became known as the go-to person in the jewelry business. Everybody in town and the surrounding community knew who Jimmy Davis was, and they liked him. Sporting a winning smile, Jimmy possessed charm, bolstered by his estimable character qualities, which allowed him to become a solid pillar in the community.

My dad was more than just the town jeweler. He was the guy who others could count on to be there when they needed him the most. Knowing that his purpose in life was to know, love, and serve God, just like the Catechism taught him, my dad did this. He lived his faith, helping others each and every day of his life.

Once his stellar reputation became firmly established, he left his managerial position at the Jewel Box to begin his own business. He named it Davis Jewelry. With three children and a fourth who came as a surprise in 1960, he needed to be his own boss. With a family of six to provide for, my dad required the extra profit margin that ownership would provide.

Although Therese was not planned, she was definitely welcomed with open arms when she was born five years after Marie. She arrived the same year that the first Roman Catholic became President of the United States. With four children ranging from age ten to infancy, we had a house full and then some.

My dad, who was somewhat political, was proud that Georgia provided John F. Kennedy with his greatest plurality of any state in the USA. I remember those years vividly and fondly.

Despite all that Jimmy Davis had on his plate, he always had time for his children. When I played Little League baseball, he came to every game, but he did more than that. His business, Davis Jewelers, sponsored the baseball team. He was proud to do it. For most parents, this would have been enough, but not for my dad. He did much more.

He also attended Berry College at night in Rome, Georgia, eventually graduating with a business degree. He wanted to be the first person in the Davis family to graduate college, so that's exactly what he did. This was a lifelong goal of his that finally came to fruition. Always active in the community, in his spare time he also became an active member of the Knights of Columbus.

Not nearly satisfied, my father sponsored nearly every community activity Cartersville had to offer. Whenever something came up, Daddy was the first person who was called. Although primarily altruistic, being this engaged in the community was also good business. It meant that Davis Jewelers would thrive.

Of all the activities he did, his pride and joy was sponsoring the high school senior prom. He did this every year. Doing so was his stellar achievement. It was the height of the social season in Cartersville. My mom loved sponsoring the prom as well. It gave her celebrity status in the community.

Davis Jewelers paid for everything at the prom. They bought the punch, the decorations, and the promotional material. Based on his wild experiences as a GI, which he did not want replicated at the prom, he even compensated two off-duty policemen to make certain the kids stayed in line.

At the prom, my mom and dad danced more than any of the kids. My parents learned to do the twist and the Mashed Potato, but they jitterbugged most of the time. It was their dance of choice. It reminded them of their youthful days right after the war. I think they had more fun than any of the students who attended.

Dancing was good exercise as well. My dad had always been fit. Although a little pudgy, he was strong and healthy, but that began to change. His lifestyle wasn't as hale and hearty as it needed to be. He continued to smoke, although he did change brands when filtered cigarettes became popular. His brand of choice was Winston 100s. Once he made the switch, believing it would be healthier, he never went back to straight cigarettes again.

*　*　*

Smoking wasn't my dad's only issue. He was plagued with digestive problems as well. Each night, to calm his sour stomach, he would drink a quart of milk and chase it down with a huge swallow of Maalox—sometimes as much as half a bottle. Mom bought Maalox by the gross. That's how badly he needed it, but indigestion wasn't even his greatest problem.

In the mid 1960s, about the time Therese began school, Dad was diagnosed with type 1 diabetes, an autoimmune disease. Although heartburn was a constant irritant, it wasn't life-threatening, not like type 1 diabetes. This was a serious medical issue.

Knowing how grave Dad's situation was, my mom put him on a rigid diet. It aimed to counter the adverse effects of the destructive disease, or at least slow down the deteriorative process. She was as watchful about what he ate as the FBI would have been about shadowing a suspected terrorist. Mom was as rigid and unforgiving as a drill sergeant, and my dad ate exactly what she told him to eat, at least when she was around.

When she wasn't, it was a different story. I know this because when my dad would pick Therese up after school, which he did often, they would routinely stop to buy an ice cream cone. Still in his mid-to-late forties, having been invincible his entire life, he continued to act like he always would be. Men can be like that. My father certainly was.

Despite these impediments, he continued to work hard, to be available for others, and to spend plenty of time with his family. Even though Therese was younger than her three older siblings, my mom and dad never slighted her. Refusing to allow her childhood to be less than ours had been, they continued to be very active with her.

One of the things they did was take her to Red Top Mountain. Located within a few miles of Cartersville, the top of the mountain had picnic tables for families, swings and slides for kids, and a majestic view at the top of the mountain. It was breathtaking. From the top, they could see all the way to Chattanooga and beyond.

Because it was relaxing and fun, they went often. By that time, we were in our early teens, so going with them no longer appealed to Claire, Marie, or me. Therese, on the other hand, loved going.

While picnicking one day, my parents met a man named Watson Coffee and his wife, Valerie. Striking up a conversation was easy for my dad. He could do it with just about anybody. The two couples ended up becoming friends.

Watson Coffee was tall, had dark hair, and was very personable. A little younger than my parents, he and Valerie hit it off well with both of my parents. Exchanging numbers, they agreed to meet the following week on top of the mountain.

Sharing lunch together the following Sunday afternoon, both families had a great time. Mentioning that they were going camping the following weekend, the Coffees asked if Jimmy and Cleo would like to join them. Because he had to work, my father declined. When he did, Watson suggested that they take Therese along with them, saying that she would be well cared for.

My mom and dad thought it would be a great idea, so they accepted. Confirming the details, my parents never realized that what they had just agreed to would change the course of their youngest child's life forever. It would impact the rest of us as well.

Victims are often already full of self-doubt,
and we make recovery harder by
laying . . . blame on them.

ANNA SALTER

Chapter 14

★ ★ ★

YOU'D BETTER NOT TELL

The predator wants your silence.
It feeds their power, entitlement,
and they want it to feed your shame.

—VIOLA DAVIS

Young girls dream of being a princess, of experiencing a life where nothing goes wrong, but many see their dreams shattered by the frequent, negative vicissitudes of life. In *Les Misérables,* Fantine has an insightful lyric that expresses the difficulties we all face beautifully: "There are storms we cannot weather."

We like to think we are strong, in control of everything. We picture ourselves as resilient, immortal, almost invincible, but that's just an illusion. One has to be divorced from reality to believe in such fantasies.

Having weathered World War II, where young men not yet having reached the prime of life were taken routinely, my father understood the frailty of human existence. He witnessed carnage and destruction on a daily basis, but there are other, less violent storms that people also cannot weather.

My mother's molestation was a perfect example. She was unable to put her sexual abuse at the hands of Lance Pervers behind her. She wanted to. She desperately tried to but to no avail. What that man stole from her adversely impacted her for the rest of her life, altering every aspect of her being. She didn't want to be an adult who threw tantrums.

Nevertheless, because of what had been taken from her, coupled with how being violated twisted her thinking, adversely affecting her self-worth, these things made her subsequent behavior predictable. Those who have never had such an experience simply cannot grasp how destructive sexual abuse can be, especially in one's formative years. Once the molestation ends, most people mistakenly assume the victim can put the events of the past in their rearview mirror and move forward, but this rarely happens. To think that it does, or even that it could be possible, is pie-in-the-sky optimism that is divorced from reality.

Like the chains of Marley's ghost, the destructive weight of a pervert's depravity debilitates the victim for the remainder of their life. In the USA, one out of every three girls are violated, and one out of every four boys. A person who commits murder robs a victim of their life. A pedophile robs his victims of their soul.

Having to counter the emotional devastation of Pervers's repeated molestation of my mother, and having to deal with its aftermath for decades, my father was well aware of how destructive pedophilia can be. Because he loved his wife as much as he did, he was always compassionate with her, as gentle as the Lord Himself would have been.

Although I didn't understand the dynamics of their relationship at the time, in hindsight I am now aware of what actually created her dysfunction and her arrested development. As a result, I have begun to view her behavior differently.

At the time, what she did was scary, the behavior of a crazy woman. Now, after gaining insight, I have a better understanding of the demons that plagued my mother's life. Because of her violation, she was unable to function the way she desired, the way she would have if her defilement had never occurred.

My father understood this. Having made a sacred marital vow to love his wife in sickness and in health, he did just that, never rejecting, never scolding, and never belittling her for behavior she had the inability to control.

With very few counseling tools available back then, and with no formal training to guide him, he did his best, achieving remarkable results. His ability to calm her down, to restore her to normalcy, was incredible. When they came out of their bedroom after one of her explosions, she was a different person, a much better version of herself.

We were always relieved to see her sane, but we knew the transformation wouldn't be permanent. At some point, without warning or provocation, the Dragon Lady would reemerge to throw a tantrum, horrifying my sisters and me in the process and scaring us half to death.

Fully aware of what was behind my mother's pathology, and having three daughters to protect, my dad was hypervigilant where Claire, Marie, and Therese were concerned. Knowing it was his job to protect them from scoundrels like Pervers, my dad kept a watchful eye out for all three of them.

Unfortunately, where Therese was concerned, he missed the warning signals, so he went to his grave never knowing what had happened to his youngest child.

My mom missed the signals too. Being concerned about my father's diabetic condition, her focus was on her husband, not on her youngest child. Neither Claire, Marie, nor I knew either. It was years before we would—decades, really.

Chronologically, Therese's abuse began in 1965, the year my dad was diagnosed with type 1 diabetes. This was also the year the first US combat troops arrived in Vietnam.

My parents let their guard down with Watson Coffee and his wife. After striking up a friendship on Red Top Mountain, neither my mom nor my dad had any misgivings about allowing Therese to go camping with the Coffee family. They thought it would be fun for Therese to "get in touch with nature," but that's not what she got in touch with.

While on the three-day trip, Watson Coffee, a man in his late thirties, raped my five-year-old sister. He didn't just molest her; he penetrated her.

Therese had no idea what was happening, but she knew she didn't like it. As young as she was, she had no sexual awareness. No five-year-old ever does—that is, unless the child has already been sexualized. Once a child has been robbed of their innocence, it can never be restored. It's gone with the wind. It's replaced by fear, shame, confusion, and a deep, never-ending sense of guilt and self-loathing.

To keep Therese quiet and to make certain she didn't tell my mom and dad what had happened, Watson convinced her that everything had been her fault. Shaming her to silence, which is the primary strategy of pedophiles, he intimidated her into compliance.

"I'm going to talk to your parents," he threatened. "I'm going to tell them what you've done."

Terrified and thoroughly intimidated, as any five-year-old would be, Therese didn't say anything to my parents. She didn't tell anybody else either. She kept it to herself, internalizing the soul-crushing consequences of her rape deep within her heart.

Her violation wasn't a one-time event either. Monthly, sometimes more often than that, the Coffees would call and offer to take my little sister camping or back to their house for an over-the-weekend stay.

Loving that this wonderful family had taken such an interest in Therese, my parents permitted this to continue, never saying no to their good friends. Because they didn't, Therese's abuse continued. She was raped repeatedly, at least once a month, from the time she was five until she was eleven.

Watson Coffee didn't just sneak off to do this. It was a family affair. There were numerous times when his wife, Valerie, watched. Enjoying the spectacle and receiving voyeuristic pleasure from it, she never lifted a finger to help my little sister. Occasionally, others were allowed to have sex with my sister as well.

Feeling a deep sense of shame and unworthiness, Therese never resisted. Instead, she came to believe that being an active participant was the role she was supposed to play. When she was told what to do, she became compliant, behaving in precisely the way her violators demanded.

As a result, her behavior at home began to change. Her thinking became increasingly twisted. Instead of the sweet little girl with a heart of gold she had always been, she became secretive, manipulative, and deeply deceitful. Her entire life became a lie, with the truth being something she was forced to conceal from everybody.

Before dropping her off at home, Watson would always warn in a threatening tone, "You'd better not tell."

She never did. Ashamed of herself, believing that she was at fault and that somehow she had been the instigator, she never considered being forthright. She wanted to tell my dad, but she never did. She was fearful that if she did tell him, he wouldn't love her anymore. She also feared that he might kill Watson Coffee. If my dad did, he would go to jail and that would have also been her fault.

This twisted thinking became ingrained in her, just like it had in my mother, so Therese began to act out. Ceasing to be loveable, she became angry and reclusive. For no apparent reason, she would either rage, throwing tantrums, or clam up and refuse to communicate with anyone.

Believing that she was manic-depressive, my parents finally took Therese to see a child psychologist. Because there weren't any in Cartersville, they drove all the way to Athens and back each week, slightly more than a two-hundred-mile round trip. They did this just to get to the bottom of what precipitated Therese's change in behavior.

During the sessions, whenever the counselor got close to the truth, Therese would simply shut down, refusing to speak. Try as they might, neither the counselor nor my parents were ever able to get her to talk. Therese simply wouldn't permit it, but it wasn't Watson Coffee that she was protecting. It was my dad.

My parents never figured out what was bothering her. Instead, they kept permitting Therese to spend time with the Coffees, believing that it was good for their daughter.

The enduring effect of my mom's molestation by the photographer was a violent storm that never seemed to end, but it was nothing like the tsunami my sister was forced to endure alone. The aftereffects for Therese were catastrophic.

My father routinely said our purpose in life was to know, love, and serve God, which the Catechism affirmed. I believe this as well. Because I do, I think that preserving the innocence of our children and grandchildren from pedophiles is an excellent way to serve God. No child should ever have to deal with what my mother and sister went through.

The long-term impact on Therese from being repeatedly raped has been devastating. She has never been the same after being victimized like that. How could she be? Being repeatedly raped for seven years damaged her for life, producing a plethora of unsolvable emotional problems.

Remaining silent for decades, in order to numb her pain, soothe her shame, and mask her disillusionment, she abused drugs and alcohol, but that's not all. Because of how twisted, perverted, and aberrant her initial experience with a man had been, instead of being attracted to normal guys when she got older, she gravitated toward what she knew best: perverts and criminals. Not surprisingly, given the experiences of her adolescence, she was attracted to degenerates. These were the types of men who seemed normal to her.

Struggling with one thing after another, Therese has never experienced a happy life. Unlike her siblings, she has never achieved fulfillment either. Her life has been a desperate attempt to simply keep her head above water, failing to do so as often as not.

Not having the slightest clue about the origin of her troubles until very recently, neither her sisters nor I have been able to help her—not in any meaningful way, not like we would have if we had known the truth. Being uninformed, we thought she was crazy—a condition we assumed she had inherited from our loony mom. Now that we know differently, I suspect things will change. I hope they will, anyway.

When I finally became enlightened, realizing the truth, I did a Google search about Watson Coffee and his wife. I discovered that both have passed away. Knowing that pedophiles never change, I'm relieved they are no longer with us. The world is a better place without the two of them in it. If you believe in God, as I do, then you know they are now paying a heavy, eternal price for their perversion, a penalty they richly deserve.

The mind is its own place and in itself,
can make a Heaven of Hell,
a Hell of Heaven.

JOHN MILTON

Chapter 15

★ ★ ★

SERVE OTHERS

A mentor enables a person to achieve.
A hero shows what achievement looks like.
—JOHN C. MATHER

In retrospect, it seems obvious that my parents should have recognized the symptoms of Therese's victimization—her withdrawal from the family, her angry outbursts, and the change in her personality—but they didn't. Everything always seems clearer in hindsight, but it rarely does when events are transpiring.

If it were easy to discern how cunning and manipulative pedophiles are, there wouldn't be much molestation and exploitation of children, but there is. Sly, cunning, and calculating, deviants like Watson Coffee and his wife stalk their prey, camouflaging their intentions. Then, when confidence with the parents has been established, and when no one would even consider their motives to be ignoble, they pounce. Once they do, they destroy their victims, leaving shattered lives in their wake with callous disregard for the carnage.

The psychological troubles that began to plague my youngest sister baffled all of us, but, since my mother's issues continued to be as guarded as the formula for Coca-Cola, there was no way any of us could put two and two together. We just assumed that where our younger sister's inappropriate behavior was concerned, she was like our mother and the apple hadn't fallen too far from the tree.

Besides, these were the wonder years for Claire, Marie, and me. We were growing up and had our own lives to lead. In some ways, with Therese so much younger than the three of us, it was like she was our stepsister— part of a second family. Her life and her interests were totally dissimilar to ours. Because we had already passed through the phases of life she was experiencing, we didn't pay as much attention to her as we should have. Now that I have become aware of what happened, I certainly wish we had been more vigilant, more questioning, and more discerning, but we weren't.

My dad, who survived the orphanage and World War II, certainly was not naïve about how evil human beings could be. Having been an eyewitness to the death camps of Hitler's Final Solution, Jimmy Davis knew exactly what people were like, but Watson Coffee and his complicit wife fooled my father. Perhaps it's because Jimmy never suspected, never even entertained the possibility, that a man and wife would jointly conspire to do such atrocious things. I don't know if that was it or not, and I probably never will.

While Coffee's deviancy was transpiring under our noses, where Claire, Marie, and I were concerned, our lives were completely normal. Although our family wasn't as tranquil as an episode of *Ozzie and Harriet*, more often than not there were similarities. When my mom and Claire would get into an argument, which they did often, the fireworks were like the Fourth of July. Whenever my mom began to string profane sentences together, knowing what was about to commence, I made myself scarce.

We did some crazy things in the '60s, but nothing untoward. During this period, the salad days of our youth, because I was my father's only son, he went to great lengths to help mold my character. Daily, he taught me the value of integrity, diligence, hard work, and doing a job right. Having been an altar boy for several years, I came to understand the value of service, but learning to do things the right way never came quickly or easily. I had to learn my lessons through trial and error.

Well aware of this, my father, who was always fair, was also never easy on me. Even before I spent a summer picking cotton or a second summer digging ditches, I worked at Davis Jewelers, doing whatever my father instructed me to do. I began my apprenticeship as a jeweler at nine years old. Technically, I wasn't old enough to work or to have a Social Security number, but that didn't matter. I worked anyway. I never felt exploited, though. Why would I? I loved being at my father's store. Those have been some of the fondest memories of my entire life.

Determined to bestow what he had learned about the jewelry business on his children, Dad made certain to teach my sisters and me everything he knew. As a result, all three of us became certified gemologists. Thanks to our dad, we had a skill that, no matter what, we could always fall back on. It's an expertise few have ever mastered.

By the time I was ten, I had already sized my first ring. You cannot imagine how proud I was, my father too. When I was just thirteen, I sold my first diamond ring. I couldn't wait to go home to tell my mom. I also learned how to engrave. This was a skill that required extraordinary precision.

One time, I was given a gold belt buckle to engrave. Being meticulous, I worked diligently to make certain the engraving was perfect. When I finished, I noticed that I had inverted the numbers on the date. Horrified by my mistake, I brought the buckle to my father to tell him what I had done.

Looking at it, he said, "No problem, Tommy. Just go in the back and sprinkle a little salt on it."

Surprised by his response, I asked, "How will that help?"

"It won't, but it will make the cost of eating your mistake a lot easier to swallow," he countered.

He meant exactly what he said. I had to pay for my mistake and, as everybody knows, gold is very expensive. From that point forward, I double- and triple-checked everything, but I learned my lesson. I never made a mistake like that again. In my business dealings as an adult, I wisely continued to double-check everything.

Teaching us the jewelry business was what Dad had to give, so he gave it, but he also wanted to make certain we learned more than how to be skilled jewelers. He was equally determined to teach us how to serve others. Once again, I had to learn my lesson the hard way.

One day, while I was in the front of the store, prepared to deal with any customers who might walk in, an old man in dirty jeans opened the door. Muddy and unkempt, he looked like he knew what he was doing. So, instead of greeting him, I continued to read my book. Passing me, he walked to the back of the store where my father was working.

A half hour later, the man left. As he was departing, my dad said, "Thanks a lot, Earle."

Turning to me a moment later, my dad grabbed my book. Looking at me sternly, with obvious displeasure, he said, "You can't judge a book by its cover." Pointing to the front door, he continued, "That's the wealthiest man in the county, and he just bought $3,500 worth of jewelry. When someone comes into the store, regardless of who you think they are, greet them." A long, awkward moment later, he added, "Do you understand me?"

"Yes, sir," I replied, and I did. It's a lesson I've never forgotten. I learned to never assume anything.

According to my dad, if I made the wrong assumption, splitting assume into three words, it would "make an 'ass out of u' and 'an ass out of me.'"

I can still hear him saying this. He was never mean about teaching me these lessons, though, just firm.

Knowing how unforgiving life can be, he did his best to prepare my sisters and me for adulthood.

He wasn't always stiff. As often as not, he seasoned his lessons with playfulness. He joked about everything. Having a great sense of humor, he frequently used me as his guinea pig. I remember one example vividly.

In the early 1970s, Atlanta had a professional ice hockey team named the Atlanta Flames. One year when they made the NHL playoffs, I bought two tickets to attend a game. It was in May, which meant it was already very warm in Atlanta. Despite the mild weather, my dad convinced me that the arena would be very cold because of all the ice. He suggested that my friend and I wear heavy winter coats to ward off the cold. So, we walked into the arena wearing parkas. Everybody else was wearing short-sleeved shirts. Seeing what we were wearing, those around us laughed, and so did my dad when I told him what happened. Knowing how ridiculous we looked, we took our coats off and sat on them. They made great cushions.

* * *

After graduating high school, where I was the fullback on the football team, in order to hone my skills to be considered for a major college program, I went to Tennessee Military Institute. While playing for Cartersville High, my dad was my biggest fan. Sitting in the stands, with a voice as loud as a megaphone, he would bellow, "Hold that line!" His admonition would always spur my teammates to do just that.

Tennessee Military Institute is located in Sweetwater, about halfway between Chattanooga and Knoxville. It's not far off of I-75. The school is frequently referred to by the locals as TMI—but not in the manner of the typical acronym. Long before those letters stood for "Too Much Information," residents near the institute called it "Ten Million Idiots." I'm not kidding. I graduated, but finishing college wasn't what I intended to do with my life. My dad was determined for me to get a degree, but I wanted to go to work and earn money.

By the time I finished being one of the Ten Million Idiots, Claire, who was three years older than me, had already married her high school sweetheart. Charles Dunn was a young man whom my sister loved dearly, but my dad didn't like him one bit. Dad never had a good thing to say about Charles, and neither did my mother.

Claire, who didn't care what either of them thought, was determined to become Mrs. Charles Dunn, despite my parents' opposition.

As you can imagine, this created tension and numerous conflicts, but Claire was no shrinking violet. By the time my older sister was in her late teens, she was formidable. Strong-willed and headstrong, she could give as good as she got in an argument. Never backing down, determined and resolute, she finally got her way. As it turned out, Claire was right about Charles. My parents weren't. Once married, they remained man and wife until his death half a century later.

★ ★ ★

Type 1 diabetes can play havoc with a person's well-being. My father's struggle with the disease was no exception. Where his health was concerned, my mom was a trooper, doing everything she could to make certain he ate well and took his medicine as prescribed. My dad wasn't the best patient, though. He continued to live his life the way he wanted, which included smoking a pack of cigarettes a day. Getting hooked while a teenager in the army, like millions of other GIs, he never kicked the habit.

As his health began to decline, he was unable to be as active in the community as he had been. Because he couldn't, business at Davis Jewelers dwindled. Finally having to close the store, my dad became the manager at a new jewelry store in Sandy Springs, located in the northernmost part of Atlanta, in the late 1960s. The store was located in a new strip mall just a few blocks south of North Springs High School.

He worked long hours to make the new venture profitable. Because the commute to Cartersville was so taxing, Dad, Mom, and Therese moved to the Atlanta area. This made things much easier for my father, but there was also a hidden benefit. With Therese in Atlanta, her weekend outings with Watson Coffee and his wife were no longer easy to accommodate. That they weren't was perfectly fine with my younger sister.

By that time, I was working in distribution for Federated Stores. Federated was the parent company for Rich's department store, Atlanta's major chain at the time. I also had a girlfriend who I eventually married. Her name was Carlene. She was a very pretty woman.

During our sixteen-year marriage, we had four children. By the time we started dating, Claire and Charles had already had their first child. She was a beautiful little girl named Mary-Claire.

Mary-Claire was the delight of her grandparents, especially to Grampus, the name Mary-Claire called my father. Now that Claire was a parent, she and my mom got along considerably better. Reminiscent of the early days of my mom and dad's marriage, Claire, Charles, and Mary-Claire spent a great deal of time with my parents. Family get-togethers were common.

One weekend in late September, Clair, Charles, Marie, Therese, and the baby were all at my parents' house for the weekend. This was just a few weeks before Richard Nixon won the '72 presidential election by a landslide.

I don't believe that weekend was a special occasion, just something they all wanted to do. Everybody was present but me. Since I was in love, I stayed with my girlfriend at her house.

On Sunday morning, September 22, 1972, with her infant fussing, Claire woke up early to take care of the baby. My father was also up. He had gone downstairs to drink a glass of milk, which was not unusual. Having significant digestive problems, he did this frequently. Knowing his routine, Claire thought nothing of it.

Suddenly, there was a loud crash downstairs, startling everyone. It was so loud that it awakened the entire household.

"What was that?" my mother shouted, sitting straight up in bed.

Responding, my father replied in a slightly exasperated tone, "That was just me." He added, "Everything is fine."

He had fallen, but he was quick to assure everyone that there was no reason to be concerned. I suspect he was more embarrassed than anything else. Continuing upstairs, he passed the room where Claire was tending to Mary-Claire.

Looking at his first granddaughter, who was the delight of his life, he said, "Listen to that little devil. She's trying to talk."

Smiling at my dad, Claire was about to respond, but before she could, he collapsed right in front of her. Horrified, rushing to his aid after putting the baby down, my sister alerted the rest of the house that Dad was not breathing.

Instantly, everyone came to our father's aid. Having been trained as a nurse, Marie took over immediately, giving him CPR. Her goal was to keep him alive until an ambulance arrived.

In the midst of the ensuing bedlam, while it was still dark outside, Claire called me.

Awakened from a deep sleep, I was surprised to hear the phone ring. Long before cellphones were invented, Carlene answered the landline at her house, wondering who would be calling at such an early hour.

Passing the phone to me immediately, she said, "It's for you, Tommy."

Surprised, I took the receiver and said, "Hello?"

"Tommy," Claire said, "Dad has collapsed. It's serious. You need to get here right away."

By her tone, which was unnerving, I knew I didn't have a second to spare. Jumping to my feet, I dressed and was out of the door in record time. Racing home in my VW Bug, I was lucky to avoid being pulled over for speeding. Since my parents' house was twenty-five miles away, even driving as fast as I possibly could, it took quite a while to get home.

While I was en route, Marie continued to provide CPR. By the time the paramedics arrived, although my father was still alive, he wouldn't be for long. When I got there, which was no more than half an hour from the time Claire called, my father had already died.

When I saw him, he was in the ambulance with a sheet covering his face. I'll never forget the horror of that sight. I can still see it in my mind's eye. It has haunted me for decades.

The paramedics did all they could, but it wasn't enough. Jimmy Davis died of a massive heart attack.

Just a month and a day past his fifty-third birthday, my dad, my hero, a giant of a man, passed from this life into the arms of the Lord. Not being able to say goodbye devastated me. Half a century later, the fact that I wasn't there when he passed away continues to bother me.

In most families, it's the mom who is the glue, the person who holds everything together, but this wasn't true in our family. It was my father. All of us, including my mom, knew it. This larger-than-life man, an American hero, a guy who bucked the odds to become everything he was ever capable of being, was gone. Our loss was catastrophic. He was irreplaceable.

My mom was heartbroken, and so were the rest of us. I couldn't imagine what our lives would be like without him.

The void his departure had created would never be filled. How could it be? I still miss him, and so do my sisters.

When he died, he left us rich, not in wealth, not in material possessions, but in estimable character qualities. This was our inheritance, our heritage, not some entitled sense of white privilege.

I wouldn't trade what I received for anything. His fathering, his mentoring, had provided me with everything I required to succeed in life, especially in business.

Four days after his death, the funeral for James Thomas Davis, Sr. was held at St. Francis of Assisi Catholic Church in Cartersville, Georgia. Being as prominent in the town as he was, loved by the community's inhabitants for decades, the church was packed. Since my dad was a member of the Knights of Columbus, many members of the order attended. All wore kilts. When their bagpipes began to play his dirge, there wasn't a dry eye in the congregation. Without question, my father, who fought a world war to ensure that those who loved him would be free, was respected by all.

Witnessing his funeral, and being part of it, made me wish my father could have been like Tom Sawyer and Huck Finn, witnessing his own funeral. No doubt he would have been touched by the outpouring of love.

This was a tough day for my mother. Having loved Jimmy Davis her entire adult life, she had hoped they would enjoy a long, rich life together. She wanted many more years with him, but that wasn't to be.

Both staying faithful to each other, they remained true to their vows for the entirety of their marriage. After my dad died, my mom remained a widow for forty-three years, decades longer than she had been married. Despite continuing to be a beautiful woman, she never entertained the thought of remarrying. Finally dying many years later, after enduring a long bout with Alzheimer's, she was buried next to my father, her one true love.

The wake that preceded my father's funeral, a venerated tradition in the Catholic Church, was equally well attended. That didn't surprise anyone. Even Watson Coffee and his wife, Valerie, came to pay their respects.

Making a point to hug my little sister, who was then eleven, I learned many years later what her rapist murmured in her ear that evening.

With a sycophantic smile on his face and feigned sadness in his eyes, he whispered, "Now that your daddy's gone, who's gonna protect you?"

The fear of death follows from the fear of life.
A man who lives fully is prepared to die at any time
MARK TWAIN

Chapter 16

★ ★ ★

MY TWO-DECADE APPRENTICESHIP

The foundation stones for balanced success are honesty,
character, integrity, faith, love and loyalty.

—Zig Ziglar

Because my dad died so young, dealing with his passing was difficult for me, just as it was for the rest of my family. Although his health had been deteriorating, since he was only fifty-three, we didn't expect him to die, and certainly not as suddenly as he did. Coming to grips with it wasn't easy. It seemed incomprehensible to all of us that he was gone, never to return.

When someone you love dies out of season, their importance escalates. That person's passing becomes totally dissimilar to a person dying at the ripe old age of eighty-eight. When a person that old dies, it's often a relief for everyone, including the octogenarian, but that's not true when it's someone who dies in his early fifties.

With Dad gone, the world for everybody in our family was turned completely upside down. For my mom, the adjustment must have been the severest. She was used to having him around on a daily basis. Having their routine end abruptly was particularly difficult. For a long while, she seemed lost, becoming quite melancholic. I think she would have liked to crawl up in a ball and retreat into her own private world and become reclusive, but that wasn't possible. She still had a troubled eleven-year-old to tend to, an adolescent who needed her mother.

Having Therese at home was good for Mom. It forced her to cook, to clean, and to tend to the needs of her youngest child. Perhaps it helped take her husband's passing off of her mind just a little, but maybe not.

To help Mom out with the care of Therese, a little more than a month after my dad's death, Watson Coffee called. He offered to drive to Atlanta and take Therese home with him for a long weekend. He thought it would help if she spent some quality time with his family.

In a concerned, consoling voice, Watson said, "We'd love to have her."

Genuinely grateful for the break from parenting, Mom responded, "That's so generous of you, Watson. I'm sure she would be delighted to come."

"Fine," he replied. "I'll drive down and pick her up after school on Friday. We have lots of activities planned. I can be there by 4 p.m."

"That will work," Mom replied. "She'll be ready. We'll see you then."

Later that afternoon when Therese came home from school, Mom, feeling certain this would be pleasant, welcomed news, told Therese she would be spending the weekend with the Coffees.

Instead of being excited, Therese had the exact opposite reaction. In a firm, perfectly clear voice, she announced, "I don't want to go."

"I think it would be good for you to get away, Therese. Besides, it's already been arranged. You're going," my mom countered.

"I don't care if it's been arranged or not, Mom. I'm not going," Therese rebutted.

"Yes, you are," Cleo pronounced, drawing a hard line.

"No, I'm not!" Therese screamed. She was equally as determined and then some. Bolting out of the kitchen, she ran upstairs, retreated to her bedroom, and slammed the door behind her.

Completely taken aback, Cleo tried her best to persuade Therese to go, begging her at first, then threatening her with loss of privileges if she continued to refuse. Nothing worked. Therese wouldn't budge. More committed to not going than her mother was in forcing her to go, Therese finally won the battle of wills. Cleo acquiesced.

Embarrassed, my mom called Watson on Thursday evening. Apologizing profusely, she told him not to bother coming.

When asked why there had been a change in plans, instead of lying, saying Therese was sick or something similar, Cleo told the truth. "I'm sorry, Watson," Mom said. "Therese just doesn't want to go."

"I understand," the rebuffed pervert countered. "Perhaps it's too soon. Maybe we'll do it another time," he added before hanging up, but there would be no other time.

Therese had finally found her voice. Although she never told Mom the reason why she wouldn't go, guarding her secret for decades, my sister never saw Watson Coffee or his degenerate wife again. These two twisted perverts were out of my sister's life for good, but the damage they had inflicted on her soul remained.

It was also in her mind, twisting her and wounding her at the core of her being. What they had done created a lifetime of dysfunction for Therese that was destined to rear its ugly head in traumatic ways years later.

If my dad had lived a while longer, although I might be mistaken, I suspect he would have persuaded Therese to come forward. Perhaps he could have coaxed her to tell the truth about what happened, but I'll never know this for certain.

All of us grieved his loss, but I think his absence was more devastating to my youngest sister than to any of the rest of us.

* * *

I missed my father terribly. Words cannot describe how much. More than half a century later, I still think about him nearly every day. As surprising as it may seem, the specific thing I missed the most was our weekly chess match. We rarely missed it. What I liked the most was, during our match, I had my dad all to myself.

We started playing chess when I was just eleven years old. We played because he was determined for me to become a deep thinker, a first-rate problem solver. Chess was the vehicle he chose to teach me how to be that kind of person. Because chess requires three-dimensional thinking and is a zero-sum game, the skills necessary to win resembled those I would need to be successful in business and in life. So, chess wasn't just a game. It was an integral part of my apprenticeship in life.

At the time, as a kid, I had no idea what my dad was doing. All I knew was I loved the game and both of us had fun playing it. I didn't understand the underlying dynamics that motivated him until many years later. When I did, I marveled at his wisdom.

He never let me win, though. That would have been counterproductive. If I beat him, which I didn't do often, I had to do it on my own.

One time, after we had been playing for about three years, he asked what I had learned from playing the game. Fourteen at that time, not used to being asked serious questions, I had to think about it for a while.

Finally, I responded, "Well, if I've learned everything you know and everything I already know, then I know more than the both of us together."

Completely taken aback by my response, which sounded like a truism Yogi Berra might have uttered, my dad laughed so hard that it brought on a coughing fit, the kind heavy smokers frequently experience.

To this day, I remember the incident vividly. More importantly, I have never forgotten the problem-solving lessons I learned from strategizing to defeat my father in our chess matches. Along with a thousand other examples of paternal guidance he bestowed on me, they have become the guiding principles in my life. Although not yet twenty when he passed, because of my two-decade apprenticeship, I was well-prepared to be on my own. I was equipped to start making a living for myself, while also providing financially for others.

Not long after my dad died, I married my girlfriend, Carlene. Shortly thereafter, even as young as we were, we began our family. In the twenty-first century, married couples often wait until their late thirties or even their early forties to have children. In the 1970s, it wasn't like that. We had our kids young, when we had the energy to keep up with them. We had four children during our sixteen-year marriage, and each one was the delight of my life. Because I was the sole provider for a family of six, I had plenty of incentive to go to work and become successful.

Having left my position as head of distribution for Federated Stores, I became involved in the construction business. I worked for a man named Tyson who had nothing to do with the chicken business. During my time with him, a construction company in Conyers, Georgia, had some excess equipment they wanted to sell. When I told Tyson about it, he wasn't interested in buying it, but I was. I could smell a profit. For me, taking a risk was my Queen's Gambit.

With my boss's blessing, I made a private investment that necessitated having two partners. We bought the equipment for $60,000. Later, at an auction in Macon, we sold it for $750,000. This meant that we each netted $230,000, after paying $60,000 for the paraphernalia. Needless to say, my two partners were pleased with me.

This deal put me in good stead with AMECO, which was the equipment arm of Fleur Daniel, the second largest contractor in the USA. This was my first big score in business, but it certainly wouldn't be my last.

Not long after this, I was in Greenville, South Carolina, looking to buy some scaffolding. Due to the heat, I was wearing a T-shirt, shorts, and tennis shoes, which was definitely not business attire. Despite this, the president of AMECO Fleur Daniel asked to speak to me. He wondered if I would be interested in buying thirty-seven containers of scaffolding that were located in Alberta, Canada.

I said that I would, but it meant I needed to find an additional $250,000 to complete the deal. To make it even more difficult, all I had was thirty days to accomplish the task. Having nearly half of the funds already, I went to work to secure the rest.

Just like playing chess with my dad, this was a high-risk, high-reward, zero-sum game that I was determined to win. Loving that the odds were stacked against me, I set to work, coming up with the money just in the nick of time. Eventually making $900,000 on the deal, my line of credit at the bank went from $100,000, which was the limit for a small-time player, to $65 million. This huge increase put me in the big leagues with all of the major players. No longer relegated to small-time deals, I established my company became established as a force to be dealt with from that time forward.

In big-time business, I began to receive sizeable rewards for my effort. Over the years, I've generated more than $250 million in business with some of these same people, creating a 22 percent gross margin in the process.

A perfect example of how I became successful occurred a few years later in Edmonton, Alberta, Canada. During the Christmas break, when there was only a skeleton crew working at a massive $1.8 billion oil project, there was a gigantic fire that burned out of control for two days, leaving nothing but destruction in its wake. My $2.4 million worth of silver galvanized scaffolding was covered in black tar, which ruined it.

Restarting the project from scratch, my scaffolding was sold for scrap metal at four cents on the dollar. Keeping careful tabs on where the metal was sent, I had it tested for strength and safety. When I discovered that it had not lost any of its strength, I offered the junkyard dealer eight cents a pound for the entire lot. Doubling his profit immediately, the man jumped at the opportunity.

Taking possession of the scaffolding, I bought two industrial-sized pressure washers and cleaned off all of the tar, restoring the metal to its original silver galvanized look. Reselling the scaffolding at nearly full retail price, I made $1.7 million in profit.

All that was required to generate this windfall was a little ingenuity and a lot of hard work. The company was so pleased with what I had done, especially since it put the project back on schedule, that they rented my scaffolding for their next project, which was a much larger one. I made $75 million on that deal—that's right, *seventy-five million*!

That I was capable of making this kind of money didn't involve white privilege, but it did involve paying attention to the lessons my father taught me as a small child. That I learned them is what made me successful.

During my career, there were plenty of stories like what happened in Edmonton. I was very successful, but none of it can be attributed to white privilege. Starting with nothing other than the skills and wisdom I had been taught by my dad, I made the most out of what I had. I didn't receive an MBA from Harvard, teaching me how to be pompous and arrogant. All I had was an associate's degree from Tennessee Military Institute, making me one of the "Ten Million Idiots."

What I did have was a two-decade apprenticeship with my father. What he taught me has proven to be far more valuable than an MBA from any Ivy League school.

Because I dug ditches, I learned that to make a profit, you often needed to get your hands dirty. Because I picked cotton, I learned that to get the job done, more often than not, pain was involved. I also learned to suffer reversals. I understood that when you make a mistake, like I did when I engraved the wrong date on that gold belt buckle, you have to pay for it. By the way, salting it didn't help.

In business, making excuses and whining about failure doesn't work. Learning from your mistakes does. Based on what my father taught me, I learned to never give up. When things didn't go my way, I didn't quit. Instead, I doubled down on my resolve to turn the situation around. Remembering my experience of ignoring the unkempt customer who was wealthy, I learned to never judge a person by their appearance. Instead, I made it a practice to respect everyone, regardless of their outward looks. As a result, I've always treated people fairly.

From playing chess with my dad on a weekly basis, I learned to think strategically. So, when others were blind to a prospect, when they could see no way forward, like when the scaffolding was covered with burned tar after the fire, I saw an opportunity. Seizing the moment, *carpe diem*, I went for the gold and made a great deal of money by taking the risk.

I attribute all of this to being Jimmy Davis's son. Knowing what was required to be successful, he provided me with the tools I needed, kind of like what Daniel was required to do in *The Karate Kid*. Just like when the young man was waxing the cars, I never suspected the purpose of what my dad taught me at the time. Now, I understand. Older and wiser, when I think about what was really transpiring back then, it always makes me smile.

As a consequence of my father's mentoring, I have achieved the American dream of becoming a wealthy man. I've earned everything. Nothing was ever given to me or handed down to me on a silver platter. What I've earned, I've earned fairly and honestly. There have never been any shortcuts, never any handouts, not for me, not for the son of Jimmy Davis.

Throughout my career, I have never cheated anyone, nor have I taken advantage of anyone dishonestly. It's not in my nature to be like that. Character counts. Believing precisely as my father did that my purpose in life was to know, love, and serve God, this has been my North Star, my guiding light, precisely like it was for him.

Because of nondisclosure agreements, I cannot go into detail about my net worth. Suffice it to say, when I was offered $200 million for my company, I turned the offer down.

> *If we command our wealth, we shall be rich and free;*
> *if our wealth commands us, we are poor indeed.*
>
> EDMUND BURKE

Chapter 17

★ ★ ★

HE'S LYING

Unfortunately, with addiction,
there's manipulation and deception.

—JEREMY CAMP

My father equipped me to be successful, not just in business but also in life. Knowing I would need to be the primary provider for my family and for many others in the future, he was relentless in his efforts to mold my character. His goal was to teach me to become a man of integrity, a man who would think of others and not just of himself. Although his strategy required a great deal of effort, it finally paid off. I became the man he intended me to be.

Starting from almost nothing, I built a company that continues to be profitable and provides rewarding employment for many others. I'm very proud of what I've accomplished. I'm sure my dad would have been as well.

I remained single after my divorce for quite a while. Then, truly smitten by a lady's beauty, wit, charm, and sophistication, I married Michelle Hayes. Everybody calls her Buttercup. Being well-suited for each other, we've had a very successful marriage, recently celebrating our twentieth anniversary. We live in Boca Raton, Florida, where we enjoy the fruits of the American dream. Although happily semiretired, we remain quite busy, especially Buttercup.

My business continues to thrive, but our family's story doesn't end there. It's true that the blessings of my father's life and leadership have been passed down successfully to his descendants, but that's not all that has been passed down.

The curse initially inflicted on my mother in the 1930s by the pedophile photographer Lance Pervers continued to wield its destructive force in our lives. The pattern has continued well into the twenty-first century, adversely impacting three generations.

Although we have been a blessed family in many ways, especially coming from such humble origins, the journey hasn't been trouble free. Nothing has ever come easily for any of us, not for the descendants of Jimmy Davis. We've never experienced anything similar to a fairy-tale ending. I wish that we had, but it certainly was not in the cards for us. Nobody ever said, "They lived happily ever after," and I doubt they ever will.

Similar to what my mother and youngest sister experienced, our family has had to weather storms we never anticipated and certainly didn't deserve. We've had more than our share of children who have been sexually violated.

No child deserves to be molested or raped, despite what the "child-attracted" crowd would have people believe. Their view, that it is somehow normal for a small portion of adults to desire children sexually, is a lie straight out of the pit of hell.

Here's why I believe this is true. My sister, Therese, having been raped herself, remained troubled. With what she experienced at the hands of Watson Coffee and his wife, how could she not be? Her subsequent travails became unavoidable.

Throughout her teenage years, she endured several bouts of alcoholism and drug abuse. While this helped her numb the pain of her exploitation, the long-term effects were devastating. Therese's personality became every bit as volatile as my mother's. I witnessed this but was unable to help. Nothing my father taught me helped either. I suppose it's because I was unaware of the troubles behind it. I was oblivious to my sister's and my mother's abuse.

The strategy of keeping these things private, of keeping them hidden, is very Southern, but it is also counterproductive. This helps the perps, no one else. Despite this, it is the first reaction for nearly all victims.

Despite what happened to her, Therese wanted to lead a normal life. In an effort to turn her life around, she started dating a very personable young man named Francis Kramer. They quickly became an item, and our family hoped he would prove to be as helpful to her as my dad had been to our mom. We welcomed Francis into our family with open arms.

To put what happened into historical perspective, this was back when Ronald Reagan defeated Jimmy Carter handily in the 1980 presidential election. It was also nearly eight years after my father's death and shortly after I married my first wife, Carlene. Anxious to become a good husband, I was more focused on my new family than on anything else. During this period, Carlene and I concentrated on building our lives together, including having and raising children.

At the same time, my older sister, Claire, and her husband, Charles, had already welcomed their second daughter, Laura. Doing their best to be supportive of our youngest sister, Claire and Charles spent a great deal of time with Therese and her new beau. The couples ate many meals together, barbequing frequently. With two children to care for, most of the events were held at Claire and Charles's house, which was amenable for both couples.

Francis was very accommodating. He even read bedtime stories to Claire's daughters while the two women cleaned up after dinner. Everybody in the family liked Francis. He was so charming that we hoped he would marry Therese. If he did, we thought he might provide her with the stability she lacked. This was what Therese desired as well. Apparently, Francis also wanted this. Things were going so well that we started calling him Uncle Francis. That's how tight he had become with our family.

Everything was going well until it didn't. One evening, Claire was about to bathe her three-year-old. While the child was sitting on the bathroom rug naked, waiting for the tub to fill up, she smiled at her mom. Pointing to her vagina, Laura said, "This is where Uncle Francis touches me."

Stunned, my sister asked Laura to repeat what she had said, which the child did. Immediately alarmed, my sister turned off the bath water. Smiling at her young daughter, she asked when Uncle Francis did this.

"He does it when he's reading us bedtime stories," Laura told her mom.

Knowing that something was dreadfully wrong, after bathing her daughter and putting her down for the night and before bathing her seven-year-old, Claire called her oldest daughter into the kitchen.

Sitting at the table, Claire smiled at her. Then she said, "You can tell me anything, Mary-Claire. You know that, don't you?"

Mary-Claire just smiled and nodded her head in acknowledgment.

Claire continued, "You know that whatever you say, no matter what it is, you will never get in trouble. You understand that, don't you?"

Again, Mary-Claire nodded.

Then my sister asked, "Mary-Claire, has Uncle Francis ever touched you in your 'private parts'?"

"No," Mary-Claire responded immediately, but, in my sister's opinion, much too hastily. To my sister, Mary-Claire's response seemed uncomfortable, perhaps even fearful.

Being cautious, Claire continued to probe. When she did, Mary-Claire finally broke down and started to cry. Holding her daughter for a long time, telling her how much she was loved, Claire allowed her seven-year-old to cry as long as was required.

When Mary-Claire finally stopped, she confirmed what her younger sister had said. Uncle Francis had been molesting both girls each time he read them a bedtime story. He did this right under the noses of the children's parents, but that's not all. He told the two girls that their parents wouldn't love them anymore if they knew what had happened. Swearing the girls to secrecy, which is the primary MO of all pedophiles, Francis manipulated the children into silence.

Fully aware of what had happened to her children, Claire knew she needed to address the situation, but she made a strategic decision to not tell her husband, not right away. Suspecting that Charles might take the law into his own hands, she wisely kept him in the dark, but just for a short period.

She decided to confront Francis on her own. Calling Therese, Claire asked if she and Francis could meet her at my mom's house, which Therese agreed to do. Enlisting the support of our mother, Claire was ready for the meeting.

When Francis and Therese arrived, Claire wasted no time confronting the pedophile, accusing him of violating her daughters.

Francis was caught completely off guard. Denying that he had done anything like that, he said, "I would never do anything to hurt your children. I love reading them bedtime stories, that's all."

Disbelieving him, in a cold, harsh tone, Claire drew a hard line. She said, "You're lying."

With the truth revealed, lacking any defense adequate enough to manipulate his way out of his deviant behavior, all Francis could do was stammer and stutter. After regaining his composure a few minutes later, he became insolent and self-righteous.

Claire, behaving like a mama bear, didn't retreat an inch. She refused to let him off of the hook, not for one second.

Angry that his good name had been questioned, Francis left in a huff. Therese followed close behind him.

Turning to my mom, Claire said, "He's lying. I know he is."

"You're right," Cleo confirmed. "He is lying." But that's not all my mother had to say. To come to her daughter's aid, to comfort and counsel her, Cleo finally came out of the closet. She told Claire everything. Finally being forthcoming, Mom explained what had happened to her as a young girl, divulging what Lance Pervers had done decades earlier.

Although shaken, Claire was grateful to learn the truth. It provided her with valuable information she needed to deal with her situation.

Later, Claire told her husband and me exactly what had happened—all of it. She also told us what had happened to my mom.

You cannot imagine how shocked and angered both Charles and I were, not just about the girls but also about Cleo. Coming to terms with all of this was difficult, but Claire's strategy, which was to keep us in the dark, had proven to be a wise one. It kept us from taking the law into our own hands.

Although Claire's strategy worked, there are no words adequate enough to describe the anger and outrage both Charles and I felt toward this evil, duplicitous, manipulative pervert.

Learning about what happened to my nieces was how I learned about my mom's molestation; I hadn't ever heard it from my father. Being a faithful man, Dad kept his promise to Mom, taking her secret with him to his grave. I wish he hadn't. I needed his wisdom about how to deal with these troubling events, but it was no longer available.

With times having changed considerably since the 1930s, when my mom's assaults occurred, Claire brought both of her daughters to counseling. This helped them considerably, but that was not the end of it. At first, Claire considered having Francis Kramer arrested. She probably should have, but she didn't. She refused to allow her daughters to be dragged through the trauma of being witnesses at a public trial, not as young and vulnerable as they were, especially the three-year-old.

Being hyper-protective, she decided against prosecution, but she refused to have anything to do with Francis Kramer ever again. So did I. Who could blame us? I don't believe either of us ever saw him again.

Our sister, Therese, came to a different conclusion. Francis finally came clean about what he had done. Telling her that he would go to therapy to correct his problem, coupled with being the master of manipulation that he was, he convinced her that their future together would be happy and positive. She believed him, and they made plans to marry.

Although we begged her not to, telling her that marrying him would rip our family apart, despite our ardent, strenuous wishes, she went ahead and did it anyway. She was that misled. Satan himself couldn't have done a better job deceiving her than Francis had.

Frankly, I couldn't believe she would be that foolish, but she was. Although invited, neither Claire, Charles, nor I attended their wedding. How could we? The thought of doing so, of sanctioning or overlooking what Francis had done, was never a consideration. To have attended would have legitimized his abhorrent behavior.

Fortunately, the couple moved to Texas shortly after getting married. Their absence was a blessing for all of us. This made it much easier for us to move on. Although the marriage necessitated nearly a permanent estrangement from our youngest sister, there was no way we would ever allow Claire's two daughters to be put into harm's way again, not where Francis Kramer was concerned.

Although I missed my youngest sister, I was glad to be rid of her husband. I thought Francis would be out of our lives forever, but this was not to be.

* * *

Years passed, several decades actually. During this period, having fathered four children, I built my business but also experienced a painful divorce. Claire's daughters, Mary-Claire and Laura, grew up. My younger sister, Marie, married and had a child of her own. Her family moved to the Houston area.

Although neither Claire nor I would have anything to do with the Kramer family, Marie did. She and her husband drove to Dallas often to spend time with them. Apparently, the two couples got along quite well. I felt uneasy about this, but at least Marie was well aware of Francis's previous behavior.

While I felt certain Therese's marriage would be short-lived, it wasn't. While continuing to live in the Dallas area, she and Francis settled down and had two children of their own. Apparently, things had worked out well for them; that is, until they didn't.

A number of years later, a young lady the Kramer family knew came forward to accuse Francis of molesting her. He had done this when she was much younger. Just a few days later, a second young woman, who was the younger sister of the first victim, came forward to accuse him as well. Filing a police report with the Rockwell County Police Department, a suburb of Dallas, officers arrested Francis Kramer for child molestation. While in police custody, at least four other young women came forward with the same accusation. In total, there were six or seven who accused him.

Denying everything, continuing to present himself self-righteously as a victim, Francis fought the charges. Being married as long as he had been, he expected Therese to stand by him, but my sister refused. She no longer believed or trusted her husband. The scales of deception had fallen from her eyes. She saw him for exactly who he was, a serial child molester. Horrified that she had believed him for so many years, sleeping in the same bed with him nightly only to learn that she had been systematically deceived throughout the entirety of their marriage, my sister was no longer willing to play the part of a fool.

She filed for divorce, but this didn't bother Francis. Knowing he faced serious jail time, he was more concerned about his impending prosecution. Coming from a wealthy, prominent family, he had excellent legal representation, but this was Texas, not New York or California. He couldn't buy his way out of what he had done.

The testimony of the witnesses, especially since there were so many of them, ensured his conviction. In 2014, he was sentenced to fifteen years in prison. Since that time, he has come up for parole twice, but one of the witnesses, the first one, continued to convince the parole board that Francis Kramer remained a threat to young girls.

The witness was correct. Pedophiles don't change. They never change. Despite what those who champion permissiveness would have people believe, perverts like Francis Kramer will always be a threat to young, naïve, innocent children.

When the explosive allegations first surfaced, Claire was crushed. She felt a deep sense of guilt for not having prosecuted Francis Kramer years earlier. Knowing that if she had, other young girls would have been spared, my sister was torn up about it.

At the same time, her first responsibility was to protect her daughters. So, who can blame her for not wanting to put them through the ordeal of a trial? I certainly couldn't, but I'm also relieved that this deviant remains behind bars, where he is destined to serve his full sentence. Prison is where he belongs.

Now divorced, my sister Therese remains troubled, but she is starting to do better. I'm thrilled about that. If my dad were still alive, I'm sure he would be as well. Family meant everything to him. It does to me too.

Despite this level of trouble, this enormous amount of adversity, the Davis family remains tight. We are a resilient lot, just like my father and brothers were nine decades earlier. Similar to them, dealing with overwhelming obstacles is hardwired into our DNA.

A family is a place where principles
are hammered and honed
on the anvil of everyday living.
CHARLES SWINDOLL

Conclusion

★ ★ ★

YOU PLAY THE HAND
YOU ARE DEALT

*The results of philanthropy are
always beyond calculation.*

—MARY RITTER BEARD

Beginning from the time I was a small child, I remember my dad saying, "You play the hand you are dealt." He was crystal clear about this, and I have never forgotten it.

A profound admonition, it may have been the most important thing he ever said to me. He maintained that it does no good to wish you were dealt a better hand or a different hand. It also meant that it would do no good to cry over your circumstances, bemoaning how unfair life has been. Sulking about your situation doesn't work either. Feeling sorry for yourself is a waste of time. Instead, you take what life gives you. Be grateful for what you have, and make the most of the hand you've been dealt.

Obviously, having had no other choice, my father was forced to do this. Instead of wishing that things were different, having no power to change his situation, either at the orphanage or having to fight his way across Europe, he did the best he could with the situation he had been given, achieving remarkable results in the process. His message—one that I'm certain I heard at least a thousand times—was clear. It became as much of a part of me as any of the answers I memorized from the Catechism as a young boy.

In my case, as the child of Jimmy Davis, along with my three sisters, we were dealt a difficult hand to play, one that did not include any white privilege, but it wasn't nearly as difficult as our dad's. Nevertheless, we had to play the cards we were dealt. That the hand was unfair, especially for the violated females in our family, didn't matter. We had to do the best we could, given our circumstances.

What we were expected to do, what Almighty God intended for us to do, remained unambiguous. His will never changes. It is for us to know, love, and serve Him—not based on what we want life to be, but on what life actually is.

For us, our earthly father was our example. There's no doubt that Jimmy Davis had been dealt a shitty hand. He was never the beneficiary of white privilege or of any other kind of privilege. Having survived the orphanage and having weathered the difficulties of being a penniless shoeshine boy and a combat veteran in World War II, by the time he was in his early twenties, he had already survived more challenges, more disappointments, and more setbacks than most would ever face. He never allowed any of his misfortunes to get him down, though.

Instead, dealing with life on life's terms, whenever he got knocked down, which happened more than his fair share, he got right back up. He did this consistently and repeatedly. That he was able to do this, more than any other aspect of his character, was what made him a special human being, an American hero. Dealing with adversity became his strength, not his weakness. He never allowed misfortune to limit his future.

A true patriot, he steadfastly believed in the American dream. He was convinced that through honesty, diligence, hard work, and a little luck, success would be inevitable, and it was. With these ingredients being the bedrock for everything he did, he believed that fulfillment was achievable.

Never whining about how difficult his situation was growing up, never blaming others for his lot in life, never considering himself to be a victim, he played the cards he was dealt masterfully, becoming an extraordinary human being in the process. Just like my three siblings, I have always been proud to be his child.

Others felt strongly about our dad as well. Those who knew him best considered him to be a solid Christian and a true patriot. Truly, it has been an honor to carry his name.

More than any other aspect of his character, his positive work ethic made my father heroic. Nevertheless, being successful and a good provider was not all that interested him. He knew there was more to life than simply getting ahead. Financial solvency was not an end in itself. There were other praiseworthy goals that needed to be achieved.

Since being successful is never a straight line upward, even when things were not going well, he never forgot that he had a higher purpose. That purpose, which he passed on to me and my sisters, was to know, love, and serve God. We heard this message from him so often that it bored us—that is, until it didn't. At some point, it became an integral part of who we were. Despite some of the obvious difficulties that threatened to derail us, we knew that to be truly fulfilled, we were required to pass our blessings along to others.

I definitely understood this. To hoard my blessings, especially after becoming wealthy, would have produced dry rot in my soul. My life would have become dominated by self-seeking greed and avarice. I saw the destruction this kind of lifestyle produced in others, and I didn't want it for myself.

While growing up in Cartersville, I remembered how involved my father had been in our community. Regardless of how busy he might have been or how taxing his situation was, he always had time and energy to help others. I witnessed his repeated outpouring of love for the community my entire life.

Once I became aware of my mother's abusive past, I respected what my father had done more than ever. Reinterpreting events from an informed perspective, I finally understood how loving, nurturing, and accepting he had been, not just occasionally, but for the entirety of their marriage. He truly loved her in sickness and in health.

Knowing this, recognizing how valuable such selflessness could be, I chose to follow in his footsteps. I made a commitment to be generous and philanthropic, rather than an unloving, uncaring, crass materialist. Having achieved substantial financial success, I was keenly aware that to be at peace with myself, to be truly fulfilled, I needed to pass my blessings along to others.

Obviously, this began at home with my four children. Setting about to help others as well has created some of the most rewarding moments of my life. Not only that, but it also made my participation in events outside of my world a hell of a lot of fun.

Like my dad, most of my philanthropic undertakings were local. Living in Roswell, Georgia, I became involved with enAble of Georgia. This was a group that helped young people who were handicapped, especially mentally challenged. Over the years, in addition to being on their board of directors, I donated at least $750,000, raising millions more for this worthwhile charity.

This might seem like it would have been enough, but it wasn't. When you are wealthy, giving money is easy. It requires very little. Often, it's even beneficial from a tax perspective. Knowing this, I wanted to give more of myself, so I did.

This was when I met Alfred. He was twenty-nine at the time. Although his IQ was no more than seventy, he was a warm and caring young man with an infectious smile. Befriending him, I included him at Thanksgiving,

Christmas, birthday parties for my children, and numerous other family events. I did this for years. He became a part of our family, a person my kids loved to see. We embraced him, and he loved us for it.

Although limited mentally, Alfred was an extraordinary athlete. He was a great bowler, but his true talent was as a golfer. He could hit the ball a mile. He was so good that I sponsored him to be in the 1992 Barcelona Special Olympics. As the event drew near, however, because there wasn't enough interest in golf, the event was cancelled.

Knowing how crushed Alfred would be, I worked tirelessly to have him included in another event. I finally succeeded. He participated in the men's doubles event at tennis. Even though tennis was far down the list of the sports Alfred was good at, because he was six foot three, he dominated, winning a gold medal with his partner.

You cannot imagine how proud he was. This was the highlight of his life. Of all the things I've accomplished, this ranks as high as any of them. I loved being part of Alfred's success. I was grateful to have worked so hard to make it happen, especially knowing that my dad would have done exactly the same thing—no matter what hand he had been dealt.

The harder I work
the luckier I become.

GARY PLAYER

Acknowledgments

Considering the complexity of a book project like this, one that I could not have completed without substantial help from others, I need to acknowledge their contributions.

Undertaking such a task seemed daunting, especially for a nonwriter like me, so that's when Tamila Kianfard jumped in to help get the ball rolling. Never backing away from what the job required, her efforts were tireless. Thank you, Tamila, for all that you did to launch this effort.

I also want to thank my sister Claire, and my two other sisters as well. Three years older than me, Claire brought memory about past events that has not only augmented mine but also frequently exceeded it.

Thanks also to Charlene Stewart for helping me manage this project and for so much more.

More than anyone, however, I want to thank my wife, Michelle, affectionately known as "Buttercup," for correcting me when I veered off course.

Finally, I want to thank Jack Watts for his skill and expertise in helping me take *An American Hero* to a higher level, providing the writing skills required to make this book become everything I ever envisioned it to be, and more.

To all of you, thank you from the bottom of my heart.

—Tommy Davis

About the Authors

Tom Davis, Jr. obtained his A.A. while playing football at Tennessee Military Institute, and later earned his G.G. degree as a graduate gemologist. Having apprenticed as a jeweler, he worked in the jewelry department at Rich's in Atlanta, doing so well that he was promoted, finally becoming the vice president of distribution and transportation. Then, at the age of thirty-two, looking to escape corporate politics, Tom began buying and selling used construction equipment.

Not long thereafter, he formed his own company, AT-PAC. During a trip to Greenville, South Carolina, at Flours Daniels Equipment yard, the president of AMECO offered Tom to purchase forty container loads of scaffolding, located in Edmonton, Alberta. He did. Succeeding in this deal, he was awarded another contract for a $1.7 billion project, establishing his business, which continues to operate profitably, even though he is semi-retired.

Tom and his wife, Michelle, both philanthropists, live in Boca Raton, Florida. An avid sportsman and big-game hunter, Tom has five children and seven grandchildren, two girls and five boys.

Jack Watts is a prolific author. Having written thirty-four books and screenplays, including nine biographies, six of them commissioned, he received his AB from Georgia State University, his MA in Church-State Studies from Baylor University, and all but his dissertation for a PhD from Emory University. Divorced, living in Atlanta, he has five children, eleven grandchildren, and four great-grandchildren.